The Master Teacher Within

By

James F. Twyman

Books by James F. Twyman

The Moses Code
The Barn Dance
Emissary of Light
Emissary of Love
Giovanni and the Camino of St. Francis
I AM Wishes Fulfilled Meditation
(with Dr. Wayne Dyer)

The Kabbalah Code: A True Adventure
(with Philip Gruber)

Love, God, and the Art of French Cooking
Messages From Thomas
The Prayer of St. Francis
Praying Peace
The Proof
(with Anakha Coman)

The Proposing Tree
St. Francis and the Animals Who Loved Him
The Secret of the Beloved Disciple
Ten Spiritual Lessons I Learned at the Mall
Touching the Divine
The Impersonal Light: Journey into I AM
Consciousness
The Nondual Universe — The Spirituality of
Enlightenment Made Simple for the Western World
The Jeshua Code
The Ten Symptoms of Enlightenment
The Richest Man In The World

ISBN: 9798386342869 (Paperback)

Table of Contents

This book is dedicated to the Master Teacher within each of us. I pray that these chapters will help you to discover this ONE within you.

Private Coaching with James Twyman

Have you ever wished that you had an experienced guide to mentor you on your journey to awakening? James Twyman offers a variety of different coaching programs, including the *Enlightenment Partner Program,* a three-month deep dive into the actual experience of waking up. During this program, you'll interact with James every day during the three-month program, including a private Zoom call once a week. There are other programs including an accelerated residential retreat in Mexico.

If you would like more information on these or any other program offered by James Twyman you can visit www.JamesFTwyman.com or www.I-AM-Awake.com. You can also reach out to James by sending an email to Namaste.Lake.Chapala@gmail.com

Namaste Village, Ajijic, Mexico

James Twyman is also the founder of one of the most exciting spiritual communities in the world: Namaste Village, a nondual, interfaith community in Ajijic, Mexico. This is a residential community with up to 50 live-in members, all dedicated to the experience you're about to discover through this book. For more information visit www.Namaste-Village.com.

Introduction

It is nearly impossible for me to describe how this book came into being since I wasn't conscious when most of it was written. Yes, my name does appear as the author of The Master Teacher Within, but in many ways, I had very little to do with its authorship. It might be easier if I explain the strange experience you're about to encounter in these pages. As unusual as it was I fully accept it as a miracle.

Two of my most recent books, The Nondual Universe and The Impersonal Light were written through a joining between my mind and a higher consciousness one could identify as God, Source, or Whole Mind. In other words, I was a full participant when the inspiration filled the pages of each volume. In both cases - as well as many others - I sensed the wisdom of this higher consciousness acting through me, but I also played an active in the entire process.

My experience with this book - The Master Teacher Within - was very different. It began with me asking a question that seemed important at the time, whatever that question might be, then typing a particular phrase that allowed the answer to pour through my mind without the input of my conscious mind. The phrase was:

I now open to the Master Teacher within and
the Whole Mind that is forever my own.

As soon as I asked a question, then typed the phrase, I fell into a sudden and deep unconscious state. When I opened my eyes five to ten minutes later, I looked down at the screen of my laptop and found a detailed answer to the question I had asked. The first few times this happened I was completely astounded, especially when I read what was typed on the screen. I had no memory of having written the words and yet the amazing clarity of the answer was undeniable. Once again, I realized I was in the midst of a miracle that my intellectual mind was unable to comprehend, but in which my soul was a complete participant.

The chapters you're about to read represent this amazing dialogue. The wisdom I recorded is perhaps the most important I've ever read, and I have the feeling it will extend far beyond my own efforts to share.

We're being guided into an experience that transcends the world we thought we live in, lifting us into the state of wholeness we sometimes call enlightenment or even Heaven. That may seem like a lofty idea at first, but as you begin to read this you may quickly arrive at the same place I did when I opened my eyes to see what the Master Teacher had shared - that we are fully held within the Perfect Mind of God, and there's nothing we can do to alter or change that.

At the end of each chapter, you'll find a poem. These poems are shared exactly as they were received - in perfect iambic pentameter (ten stressed and unstressed syllables in each line). I realized that the poems were meant to present the same information found in each chapter from a different angle or perspective. Perhaps you'll hear the message through the text or dialogue, or maybe the poem will reach your heart even quicker. Drink them in and let them saturate your soul.

Many will remember that the inspired messages received by Helen Schucman while scribing A Course In

Miracles were also received in perfect iambic pentameter. This seems to be the language of the Christ Mind, and I'm amazed and overwhelmed that a similar phenomenon happened in my own experience.

There's one other part of this story that seems important to mention.

In 1992 a man named Charles Buell Anderson changed my life forever. I heard about Master Teacher (as he was called by his followers) from several friends, but it was only when I listened to a cassette tape from one of his public sessions that I knew I had to meet him. I had never experienced anyone that expressed himself with such certainty, such clarity, and such a strong spiritual conviction. It was clear that he wasn't talking about something he believed in his mind, but something he knew from direct experience. I wanted the same direct experience, so as soon as I found someone who could drive me from my home in Chicago to Endeavor Academy in the Wisconsin Dells where he lived and taught, I made the trip.

The two years I spent living at Endeavor Academy under the guidance of Master Teacher were the most important of my life. He was my Great Awakener, the man who grabbed me by the scruff of the neck and pulled me out of the ordinary world into the unyielding experience of whole-mindedness.

It wasn't always gentle. Master Teacher had very little patience for the slippery tricks of the ego or the pretense of imaginary enlightenment. He was like a Zen master with a large wooden stick ready to whack my underside if he noticed me, or anyone else for that matter, diverging from the direct experience of singularity. He seemed to be a skilled surgeon who was able to see through the body to the cancer within, then with one quick movement, excise it from its hiding place. It wasn't what I expected but it was exactly what I needed, and to this day I feel such gratitude for his guidance.

Now back to the scribing of this book.

The first time I woke up from the unconscious channeling I described earlier, I felt the undeniable presence of my teacher, as if he was sitting right beside me. It was the feeling of perfect clarity he always exuded, very different than the intellectual belief most of us experience. We may believe what we hear or read, but to KNOW the Truth with unwavering certainty is the real goal of our spiritual journey. As I read the paragraphs that appeared on my computer screen I heard his voice, the same voice I remembered hearing when I pushed "play" on my small tape recorder decades earlier. I didn't waste any time because I wanted to know if this was really him or just the echo of my own inner consciousness masquerading as the man who left his body in 2008. I typed out this question:

> *"Who wrote these words? Are you coming through me or is something else going on that I don't understand yet?"*

I suddenly fell into a state of unconsciousness and when I opened my eyes again these words were on the screen:

"You're falling into the same trap you always fall into, the idea that there's a difference between the "you" that God loves and the "me" you try to separate from that same love. The instant you realize that there is no difference - except the differences you create in your own mind - will be the same instant you realize that the Master Teacher is within you, not outside. You may decide to believe that the consciousness you experienced in Wisconsin found a way to re-insert itself into this present moment, but you'd be wrong. The Voice for Christ is revealed in this present moment and speaks through any consciousness that claims it. The only question for you is will you choose to claim it Now? Since Now is the only moment it's possible to claim reality, the answer must be yes no matter how you choose to experience it. So stop messing around with ideas like "who" or "why". Concern yourself with only "YES" and "NOW", then you'll lift above the limitations of belief into the timeless Reality where I AM and where you're standing right beside me."

And that's how this amazing dialogue began. Whenever I asked a question, followed by the decision to open to the Master Teacher within, I became unconscious and the most amazing information I've ever read came streaming through. But just as my teacher said:

"The Voice for Christ speaks through any consciousness that claims it."

It's speaking through you as well, and you don't even have to fall into a state of unconsciousness to receive the same insights. All you need to do is open your mind and heart to receive that which God always offers - the Truth that is forever True. I hope this book helps you access the same wisdom I received, and in doing so, your life will never be the same.

Note: If you would like to hear recordings from the Master Teacher sessions in Wisconsin, you can visit: www.themasterteacher.tv. I strongly recommend the audio recordings.

The Master Teacher

The Power of Love

It's clear that we're all reaching toward the experience of love, though we usually do so clumsily. I want to know and comprehend the essence of love and my longing for it. I want to experience myself as One with the Source of all love.

I now open to the Master Teacher within and the Whole Mind that is forever my own.

To accomplish this you must be willing to give everything To love, THROUGH love, and AS love. Only then will you realize that Love is all there is. This is the absolute, uncompromised lesson you're here to learn, no matter how difficult it may seem: Love is all that exists in the universe. Embrace this fully and you will know, not with just your mind but your Whole Self, that it has always fully embraced you.

Let's look at some of your ideas of love and see if you can penetrate the armor you've designed to hide from its revelation. Love is often thought of as a feeling that you experience, something that you fall into or out of, and something that can be lost or found. True love is much more than a fleeting emotion. It's a choice, a commitment, and a way of being. To truly love, you must be willing to give everything you have, not just to another person, but to love itself. This means opening yourself up completely, giving without reservation, and surrendering to the power of love within you.

Through this power, you can experience the world in a whole new way. When you approach every situation with love, you're able to see the beauty and potential in all things. Love helps you connect with others on a deeper level, to understand their perspective, and to show compassion and kindness even when it's difficult. Love also allows you to be vulnerable and to express your True Self, rather than hiding behind walls and masks.

As you learn to love more deeply, you begin to recognize that love is not just a feeling, but a force that permeates everything in the universe. Love is the energy that creates and sustains life, the force that brings people together, and the power that transforms the world. When you start to see love in this way, you realize that it's all around you and that you're part of something much bigger than yourself.

To "*love as Love loves*" (which is just another way of saying to "love as God loves") means to embody the essence of love in everything you do. This means living with kindness, compassion, and empathy, and treating ourselves and others with respect and dignity. When you *love as Love loves*, you become a beacon of light in the world, radiating positive energy and inspiring others to do the same.

However, *loving as Love loves* requires you to confront your fears and limitations. You must be willing to let go of your ego, your judgments, and your attachments in order to become more fully immersed in love. This requires you to be open, honest, and vulnerable with yourself and others, and to trust in the power of love to guide you on your journey.

Ultimately, the only way to truly understand the power of love is to give everything to it. This means surrendering yourself completely, letting go of your fears, your doubts, and your insecurities, then trusting that love will lead you where you need to go. When you give everything to love, you become an instrument of its power, and you can experience the beauty, joy, and wonder of life in a whole new way.

In the end, you come to realize that love is all there is. It is the source of everything in the universe, the energy that connects us all, and the force that guides you on your journey. To truly love, you must be willing to give everything to it, embrace it fully, and trust in its power to transform your life and the world around you.

All you need to do is remember the Absolute TRUTH of what is Absolutely TRUE: Only love is REAL!

To truly love you must give all you own,
Through love, as love, a single thought to hone.
This lesson's hard, but it must be well-learned,
For love's the only truth that's truly earned.

In this universe, love's the only sound,
Nothing else exists nothing all around.
Embrace it fully, let it fill your soul,
And love will make you feel completely whole.

Let go of fear and every selfish thought,
For love's the only thing that can't be bought.
It's always been here, waiting just for you,
To show the light that is forever true.

So open up your heart and let it in,
And let love be your guide, your closest kin,
For when you love, you'll see it all so clear,
That love is all there is, it's always here.

All is in One and One is in All

Words never seem to come close to the experience I'm seeking. Speak to me of the experience that rests behind all words and concepts.

I now open to the Master Teacher within and the Whole Mind that is forever my own.

Anything that is shared by a consciousness fully enveloped in Truth is True, even when it's not accurate. In other words, a Whole Mind uses the tools set before them, even when those tools are dull. They use words and concepts like clay, molding them into an image that reflects what they see. But the image is not the reality, just as the reflection of the sun on a pond is not the sun. Don't cling to the words but dissolve into the reality that rests behind them. Then you'll know that you are that same reality.

My teaching is this: "All is in One, and One is in All." If you try to understand this with your mind you'll be lost, but if you allow your soul access to these words, you'll realize that being lost is impossible. How can anyone be lost when they're wholly contained within the One? How can anyone be separate from the inseparable source of ALL? The human mind can never grasp this reality, but your Whole Mind has never lost access to it. You have but denied yourself, but reality has never denied you.

This is all you need to know. The rest are minor details.

When you fully embrace the Truth, you tap into a consciousness that transcends the limitations of your individual mind. This consciousness allows you to see beyond the illusions of the physical world and to connect with the deeper reality that underlies everything. In this state, anything that you share is inherently True, regardless of its accuracy or the tools you use to convey it.

A Whole Mind is not limited by the boundaries of language or concepts. It uses whatever tools are available to create a reflection of Truth that resonates with the listener. This reflection may not be an exact replica of the Truth, but it captures the essence of it in a way that the listener can understand. The words and concepts you use are like clay, moldable and flexible, and a Whole Mind shapes them into a vessel that holds the Truth.

The image you create is not the reality itself. It's merely a representation, a reflection, of the Truth that you have glimpsed. Don't cling to the words or the concepts you use to convey this Truth. Instead, look beyond them, into the deeper reality that they point toward. When you dissolve into this reality, you become One with the Truth, and you realize that you are the same reality you seek.

The teaching that "All is in One, and One is in All" is a Truth that transcends the limitations of the human mind. It cannot be fully understood through intellectual analysis or logical reasoning. It can only be accessed through the soul, the deeper part of yourself that is in direct connection with the Whole Mind. When you allow your soul to access these words, you realize that being lost is impossible, for you're always contained within the One.

The inseparable source of All is a reality that you'll never fully grasp with your individual mind. It's a reality that can only be accessed through your wholeness, the consciousness that transcends the limitations of the physical world. You may have denied yourself access to this reality, but it has never denied you. It's always there, waiting for you to awaken to it.

The realization that you are One with All is all you need to know. It is the fundamental Truth that underlies all other truths. The rest are mere details, the tools we use to navigate the physical world. They're important, but they're not the ultimate Truth. When you focus on the One, you see beyond the details, and you connect with the deeper reality that is your true home.

To live in the consciousness of being a Whole Mind is to live in a state of constant connection with the One. It's to see past the illusions of the physical world and to connect with the Truth that underlies everything. It's a state of being that transcends the limitations of your individual mind and allows you to experience the fullness of who you truly are.

In the end, the Truth is not a destination you can reach through your intellect or your senses. It is a state of being that you can only access through your Whole Mind, the consciousness that transcends the limitations of the physical world. When you fully embrace this Truth, you realize that anything that is shared by a consciousness fully enveloped in Truth is True, even when it's not accurate.

The Truth envelops all within its grasp,
And anything it touches Truth shall clasp,
Though not accurate shared consciousness reigns,
And tools set before them Truth still sustains.

Concepts like clay are used to mold and shape,
An image that reflects what eyes may gape,
But still, the image is not what's behind,
The reflection is not what you will find.

Do not hold tight to words, nor cling to thought,
For the reality, the frame is not caught,
Dissolve, and all that is left will be clear,
Reality itself will then appear.

"All is in One and One is in the All,"
My teaching is simple yet so hard to call,
The mind may struggle but the soul will know,
Being lost is impossible to show.

How can one be lost when all is contained,
Within the One from which all has been gained,
The human mind may fail to grasp the truth,
But the Whole Mind knows it from days of youth.

It's just ourselves we've denied and forgot,
Reality has never left us caught,
In the embrace of One, we shall all be,
For One is All and All is One, you'll see.

Two Types of Desire

Desire and longing have always been important parts of my own spiritual life. But some people ask why it's important to long for something that's already true. In other words, if we're already whole and enlightened, why do we need to long to experience that reality?

I now open to the Master Teacher within and the Whole Mind that is forever my own.

There are only two types of desire: the desire for what is and the desire for what could never be. Until now your desire has been focused only on illusions which is why nothing in this world could ever satisfy you. Now your only goal is to turn wholly away from those same illusions toward Reality itself.

And what is this Reality? It is the knowledge and the experience that your holiness cannot be threatened or compromised, and that you remain forever as you were created, whole and complete. It is the same as knowing that only love is real and everything that seems to challenge that fact is nothing more than a distraction from reality.

You've come to the point where distractions no longer serve you. You've arrived at the borderland, a step away from your true home, where you can make a final choice: either to stay in the world of dreams where you're never satisfied, or turn back toward love, the love that never turned away from you.

The impossible remains impossible forever. There is no time in which the impossible becomes possible just because you want it to be. So give up your endless search and desire for that which could never be and turn toward the One that knows who you really are. Now that you've come to this borderland you can rest for a moment before taking that final step.

Look around and see the souls that have gathered here with you, all knowing that their holiness is assured by God. This is the moment you've been waiting for, the only moment that could ever truly exist, the holy instant when you step back into Heaven.

As you stand at the borderland, you may feel unsure about how to take the final step toward love. But remember, you are not alone in this journey. The souls that stand around you have also made the choice to turn toward reality, and they're here to support you as you make your decision.

In this moment, it may be helpful to reflect on the illusions that have led you to this point. Perhaps you've chased after material possessions, or sought validation from others, only to find that these things never truly satisfied you. By recognizing these as illusions, you can begin to let go of them and turn toward the truth.

At the same time, it's important to remember that turning toward Reality does not mean you'll no longer experience challenges or difficult emotions. Life is not always easy, but by anchoring yourself in the knowledge of your uncompromised holiness, you can face these challenges with greater resilience and peace.

It may also be helpful to seek out resources and support as you continue on your path toward the experience of Reality. This could mean finding a spiritual community, seeking out teachers or mentors, or simply surrounding yourself with friends and loved ones who share your values.

As you take that final step into the Ioly instant, you'll experience a sense of deep peace and joy. This is a sign that you're aligned with your true nature, and that you're in harmony with the love that created you. Remember to hold onto this feeling as you move forward, and continue to make choices that align with your deepest values.

Ultimately, the choice to turn toward reality is a choice for happiness, peace, and fulfillment. It's a choice to let go of the illusions that have held you back and embrace the truth of your own holiness. Take that final step with confidence and trust, knowing that you're supported by the love that surrounds you.

In life we have but two types of desire,
One for what is, one for what can't transpire.
Until now you have sought mere illusions,
Leaving you empty in your solutions.

But now you've set a goal to turn away,
From false dreams that have caused you such dismay.
Toward Reality that's always been there,
One that shines with truth beyond such compare.

In this mind your holiness can't be touched,
Remaining forever whole and untouched,
Whole and complete no threat or compromise,
Only love is real all else just a guise.

So let go of the doubts that you have known,
Embrace Reality, let love be shown.
For in this Truth find a peace that's so pure,
A joy that's lasting, everlasting cure.

Uncompromising Truth

I know that Truth is always True and that illusions are projections of our false impressions about ourselves. Why is it so difficult for us to realize this Truth if it's so apparent and simple?

I now open to the Master Teacher within and the Whole Mind that is forever my own.

Anything that is absolutely True is absolute and unchangeable. If Truth were subject to change it would no longer be True, and the absolute nature that extends from Truth would be compromised. A Whole Mind knows one thing: the Truth within has never been compromised and the instant you choose to be as uncompromising with this Truth as it is of you, you'll burst into a High Light experience wholly unlike anything you've known before.

In reality, this experience, because it is unchangeable and unchallengeable, is already within you, but you've erected imaginary barriers that seem to block the Light that never fades. But because these blocks are imaginary they have no lasting effect, though you do have the ability to stretch out the seeming effect of that choice so it appears to be a very long time. In reality, it was only an instant and was over a very long time ago.

The concepts of separation only last as long as you want them to. The escape from fear is as simple as choosing only love regardless of the appearance of illusions. Choosing only love means choosing only what is Real rather than attempting to choose against Reality. Choosing against Reality has no effect because illusions have no power. They seem to have power because you've projected them onto what appears to be outside yourself onto a world you created in your mind. The instant you stop projecting your illusions onto a world that exists only in your mind you'll instantly perceive your true home, or the Heaven you never left except in your imagination.

My only goal is to get you to open up your spiritual eyes and see where you are. Do you realize that this is the simplest decision you could ever make, if only you would choose to make it? The idea has already come into your mind but you instantly dismissed it because the goal seems so far away. Heaven seems so far away from you. If you only realized that Heaven is everywhere you'd be able to relax and release "nowhere". Did you catch that? Does releasing nowhere or nothing have to be difficult? Releasing that which has no true effect could be the easiest thing you've ever done if only you would try. My job is to convince you of the simplicity of this decision, then encourage you to make it. The instant you do finally make this decision will be the same instant it's made for ALL because ALL, or everything that is Real, is contained within you now and forever.

In other words, the only one who needs to awaken from the dream is you. Does that sound impossible? The instant you accept this, the world you've created until now will seem impossible. You'll realize that separation from the source of ALL love is an impossibility the Real World could never endure. You seem to have split from that world but it has never split from you.

This is my only teaching: reality has never and could never forget who you really are. Now it's yours to relax into this unchangeable vision of holiness. Begin by giving it away to everyone you meet, especially the one who seems to be most distant. This is why forgiveness is the key to salvation because it bridges the imaginary gap between you and anyone you perceive to be outside of You. There is no one outside the wholeness which remains forever whole. This is your salvation and it's being offered to you every moment. Receive this gift NOW, the only time it could possibly be received.

The Truth is not something that can be learned or acquired, but rather it's something that must be recognized. It's the essence of your being, the very core of who you are. The Truth is not something that you can attain through any external means, but rather it's something that you must discover. The Truth is absolute and unchangeable, and it's always present within you. It's your task to recognize and accept it. That is all.

You seem to be searching for something in this life, something that evades you, and you always look in the wrong place hoping to find it. You look to external things such as material possessions or relationships, hoping that they'll bring you the happiness and fulfillment you seek. However, these things can never truly satisfy you because they're not the Truth. They are temporary and fleeting, and they'll eventually pass away.

To find what you're really looking for you must turn away from external symbols of reality, then look within where Reality is truly found. It's a deep and profound realization that we're all connected, that we're all One. It's the recognition that we're not separate from each other or from the world around us, but rather an intimate part of the same Divine consciousness.

The journey to discover the Truth within yourself can be challenging, but it's also incredibly rewarding. It requires a willingness to let go of old beliefs and patterns of thinking that no longer serve you. It requires a willingness to be open to new possibilities and to trust in the process of life.

One of the keys to discovering the Truth within yourself is to let go of your attachment to the past and the future. You must learn to be fully present in the moment and to trust that everything is unfolding exactly as it should. When you let go of your need to control everything, you begin to relax into the flow of life and allow the Truth to reveal itself.

The Truth is not something you can intellectualize or understand with your mind. It's something that you must experience on a deep and profound level. It's a feeling of peace, love, and wholeness that fills you up from the inside out. It's the recognition that you're not separate from anything, but forever part of the same Divine Consciousness.

The journey to discover the Truth within yourself is a journey of self-discovery and self-realization. It's a journey of learning to love and accept yourself fully, exactly as you are. It's a journey of letting go of your fears and doubts and trusting in the infinite wisdom of the universe.

The Truth is not something that can be taught or learned, but rather it's something that must be experienced. It's a feeling of deep inner peace and joy that comes from knowing that you're exactly where you're meant to be. It's a feeling of wholeness and completeness that comes from recognizing that we're all connected and part of the same Divine consciousness.

When you fully embrace the Truth within yourself you begin to live your life in new and powerful ways. You begin letting go of your fears and doubts and trust in the infinite wisdom of the universe. You start to live with a sense of purpose and meaning, knowing that you're here for a reason and that you have something valuable to contribute to the world.

The Truth is absolute and unchangeable, and it's always present within you. It's your task to recognize and accept it. The journey to discover the Truth within can be challenging, but it's also incredibly rewarding. It requires a willingness to let go of old beliefs and patterns of thinking that no longer serve you, and a willingness to be open to new possibilities and to trust in the process of life. When you fully embrace the Truth within yourself, you begin to live truly, which is to say, LOVE TRULY.

In Truth's absolute nature, it is clear,
Unchangeable, beyond all doubt sincere,
For if it changed its name would be untrue,
And its power would be compromised too.

A Whole Mind knows one thing and that is fact,
That Truth within will never lose its tact.
When you choose to be uncompromising,
You'll burst into Light truly surprising.

This Light experience is already yours,
Imaginary barriers shift their cause,
But they have no power, they're just a lie,
And you of course can choose to make them die.

It may seem like time stretches out so long,
As if your long journey all seems so wrong,
But in truth, it was just an instant's play,
A moment passed, long ago, far away.

So don't be fooled by barriers' illusion,
Don't choose to stay in states of confusion,
For Truth is absolute, forever free,
And in its Light, you'll finally choose to see.

I AM That Mind

There is only one Mind in the universe, the Mind of God. I have no doubt about that. But how does the journey into that Mind begin?

I now open to the Master Teacher within and the Whole Mind that is forever my own.

The Mind that is ONE with all Reality is also ONE with every manifested form that extends from that Reality. I AM that Mind. You are that Mind. That Mind is all there is.

It's easy to accept this mentally, but the full integration of Reality comes only from a full-hearted devotion to the Source of all Reality. This inner movement of Divine Will is not only felt but can be fully realized, and as long as you remain cocooned within that Will or Divine Frequency you're safe from all illusory forms.

You can begin your journey into this timeless space through supreme acts of surrendering to the Real. This is followed by true humility, which is very different from the ego's idea of being humble. To the ego, humility is a form or a degree of guilt, while the soul perceives humility as a complete release from guilt. The ego denies its blanket of guilt by propping up the separate-self, making it appear ominous and large, while the soul affirms Reality by emptying the self and focusing only on wholeness. This is where the Whole Mind eclipses the split-mind and establishes itself as the immovable center of ALL Reality. The personality becomes a translucent veil rather than a thick curtain. It, along with the body, exists without existing, constantly phasing in and out of the world of form. A Whole Mind moves without moving to the degree that anyone lost in the web of illusions feels the promise of release.

The journey to the timeless space of Whole-mindedness begins with the recognition that the separate-self, with all its illusions of power and control, is ultimately futile. The ego's attachment to the idea of self is what creates the veil of separation from the Source of all Reality. True humility, which involves surrendering the ego's attachment to self, is the key to removing this veil and allowing the Whole Mind to emerge.

Surrendering to the Real is a supreme act of faith, trust, and devotion to the One Reality that underlies all existence. It involves recognizing that the ego's sense of control is illusory and that true power comes from aligning one's self with Divine Will. This act of surrender allows you to let go of all the limitations and illusions of the ego and open yourself to the infinite potential of the Whole Mind.

Whole-mindedness is not something that can be intellectually understood or grasped through the limited perspective of the ego. It can only be experienced through a deep and total integration of Divine Will into your being. This integration involves a complete letting go of the ego's attachment to self and a full-hearted devotion to the Source of all Reality.

As you become more fully integrated with the Whole Mind, the ego's illusions begin to lose their grip. Your personality and body become transparent, no longer seen as separate and distinct from your Whole Mind. Instead, they are experienced as part of the seamless whole of

Reality, constantly phasing in and out of the world of form.

A Whole Mind is the immovable center of Reality, the source of all power and wisdom. It's the wellspring of creativity, inspiration, and transformation. It's the place where the individual self merges with the Universal Self, where the boundaries between self and other, subject and object, dissolve into the boundless expanse of the Whole.

The journey to Whole-mindedness is not without its challenges. The ego's attachment to the self can be stubborn, and the illusions it creates can be convincing. But as long as you remain cocooned and protected within Divine Will, you're safe from all illusory forms. The Whole Mind is a refuge from the illusions of the world, a place of peace and tranquility.

A Whole Mind is not something that can be attained through effort or willpower. It's not a goal to be reached or a destination to be arrived at. Rather, it's a state of being, a way of existing in the world. It's a perspective that arises naturally from a deep and abiding connection to the Source of all Reality.

When you finally achieve this state of consciousness the concept of "other" completely disappears. Your community and mighty companions serve a purpose, yes, but when that purpose is fulfilled they dissolve into the Wholeness you know yourself to be.

Whole-mindedness is not an end in itself but rather a means to a greater end. It's a way of opening yourself to the infinite potential of Divine Will, of aligning yourself with the flow of the universe. It's a way of participating in the ongoing creation and evolution of Reality.

Whole-mindedness is the ultimate state of integration with the Source of all Reality. It's a state of being that arises naturally from a deep and abiding connection to Divine Will. It's a state of existence that's characterized by transparency, unity, and boundless creativity. The journey to Whole-mindedness is not an easy one, but it is simple if you're willing to let go of the illusions of the ego and devote yourself fully to the Real.

Mind that is ONE with all Reality,
Is also ONE with all totality,
I AM that Mind, of course, and so are you,
Whole, complete reality pure and true.

To fully integrate you must devote,
To the Source a true full-hearted remote,
Divine Will, felt and fully realized,
All illusory forms are thus neutralized.

A journey to this timeless space begins,
Through supreme surrender free from all sin,
Different now from ego's humble disguise,
Release from guilt and unifying ties.

Ego denies its guilt by propping up,
The separate self thus appears ominous.
The soul affirms Truth emptying the self,
Center of All establishing itself.

The personality translucent veil,
No longer curtain but a gentle sail,
Without existing in a constant phase,
A Whole Mind moves without illusion's maze.

Our True Identity

The quest to know who we are is primary in the world. It's also clear that most people look outside themselves to find the answer to that question. What advice would you give that would help shift the focus from looking outside to looking within?

I now open to the Master Teacher within and the Whole Mind that is forever my own.

If you ask someone who they are they'll likely answer with a series of descriptions that describe what they do or how they live. This, after all, forms the basis of their identity. If you continue by asking more detailed questions they'll describe their job, their home, their family, or their past. If you ask them to describe these things in even greater detail they'll pick certain facts they think you'll enjoy or aspects of their lives that might win your approval. Deeper and deeper they dive, and very quickly they reach the bottom of the tiny pond that forms their identity.

But there is another way. If someone asks you who you are, hold still and look deep into their eyes. Resist the urge to identify with what you do, or where you live, or any details about your family, and an infinite ocean will instantly appear before you. This ocean has no bottom and extends into eternity. In these infinite depths, you'll find your Self, radiant and whole, beyond any definition or conceptual form. The only words that will escape your lips are "I AM THAT." People will ask you what "THAT" is and they'll expect you to describe the manifestations of your experience. "I AM what I was and what I shall forever be," you'll say, and the person asking the question will walk away confused. And yet a seed will have been planted within their heart that will begin to grow, in-perceptively at first, but your single dedication to reality will nourish the roots of their lives until they themselves repeat what they heard escape your lips: "I AM That."

That is all and that is all there will ever be. This experience spreads like the rays of the sun at dawn, and there's no doubt that the light has come.

When you identify with your external circumstances, you limit yourself to the transient experiences that make up your life. These experiences are constantly changing, and as a result, so is your sense of Self. When you identify with the infinite ocean within you, you connect with a part of yourself that is unchanging and eternal. This deeper sense of Self is not defined by any external factors but is grounded in the experience of being.

The experience of "I AM THAT" is a spiritual experience that transcends language and conceptual thought. It's a state of being that's beyond words, beyond explanation. When you connect with this aspect of yourself, you tap into a source of unlimited potential and creativity. You become free from the limitations of your mind and the confines of your physical body.

The experience of "I AM THAT" is not limited to a select few. It's available to anyone willing to look within and connect with their True Self. It's not something that can be acquired through external means, such as possessions or accomplishments. Rather, it's something that can only be discovered within yourself.

The greatest obstacle to discovering your True Self is the illusion of separateness. You often see yourself as an isolated individual, separate from the world around you. When you identify with the infinite ocean within, you recognize that you're not separate from anything or anyone. You're part of a larger whole, interconnected with all of life.

The experience of "I AM THAT" is not a one-time event but a continual unfolding. As you continue to connect with your True Self, you deepen your understanding of who you are and what you're capable of. You discover new levels of consciousness and expand your sense of Self.

Connecting with your True Self is not always easy. It requires you to confront your fears and let go of your attachments. It means stepping out of your comfort zone and facing the unknown. But the rewards are great. When you connect with your True Self, you experience a sense of peace, joy, and fulfillment that cannot be found in external circumstances.

The experience of "I AM THAT" is not a solitary one. When you connect with your True Self, you become more connected to the world around you. You see the interconnectedness of all things and recognize your role in the larger picture. You become more compassionate and understanding of others and are able to approach life with a greater sense of purpose.

Discovering your True Self requires a willingness to look within, confront your fears and limitations, and embrace the unknown. But the rewards are great. When you connect with your True Self, you tap into a source of unlimited potential and creativity.

The experience of "I AM THAT" is not a religious one, but it is a spiritual one. It's a recognition of the deeper Truth that lies within us all. It's a reminder that you're more than your physical body and external circumstances. It is a call to look beyond the surface and connect with the infinite ocean that lies within each of us.

The experience of "I AM THAT" is not a fixed state but a dynamic one. It is a continual unfolding that requires you to remain open and receptive. You must be willing to let go of your attachments and embrace the unknown. You must be willing to challenge your beliefs and expand your understanding.

When you identify with the infinite ocean within, you connect with the unchanging and eternal Reality that is forever One. This deeper sense of Self is not defined by any external factors but is grounded in the experience of being. The experience of "I AM THAT" is a spiritual experience that transcends language and every definition the split-mind can hold. Only the Whole Mind grasps this Reality, and that is who you are now and forever.

Resist the urge to cling to earthly ties,
To cling to what you do or where you dwell,
And open up your heart to boundless skies,
Where oceans deep contain eternal swells.

This ocean has no bottom and no end,
And stretches out into eternity,
Where you'll discover Self-complete and blend,
Beyond all labels pure Divinity.

The words that leave your lips will be concise,
"I AM THAT", the only words you'll say,
And those who ask will find no real advice,
For "THAT" eludes description in every way.

That seed will grow with roots that delve down deep,
Nourished by your quest for reality,
'Til one day they too will wake from their sleep,
And in their hearts they'll say with clarity:

"I AM That", a mantra echoing strong,
A universal truth that all can see,
A holy breath that spreads like this bright song,
A light that comes with love to set us free.

A Resolute, Unwavering Focus

Probably the hardest thing for us is to put our complete focus on one thing at the exclusion of all else. Why is this so important and how can we achieve this level of intent?

I now open to the Master Teacher within and the Whole Mind that is forever my own.

A resolute, unwavering focus on what is true dispels every illusion.

Read those words again because they offer you a total escape from the split-mind's assumed dominance. If this is true, and I promise you it is, then you've been given the key that opens the door to the direct experience of your unchallenged wholeness. Do not look back upon the world the split-mind loves. Every relationship and need you have is automatically protected and resolved if you hold this focus. Do not waver from it for even an instant and you'll open your eyes to such a glorious vision that the world will dissolve before you. If this is truly what you want, which is what you've claimed, then you hold the key that unlocks the only door you have yet to open.

That which you are exists forever while that which you are not is a dream. Dreams will never become real just as reality will never become a dream. But this you do not believe and that's why you're so confused. Your perceptual mind has tried to claim that which can never be claimed. It cannot be claimed because it is not in the Mind of God, and anything that is not in the Mind of God is a dream, unreal, and without substance.

Confuse these two no more. You have dreamt of impossible worlds with impossible problems and unlikely solutions, but none of them were real. The Real World is forever protected from your strange illusions, so seek only the door that leads into your Eternal Home. It's right in front of you this and every moment but it only appears when you turn your back on the world that has never given you what you really want.

From this moment on you cannot claim ignorance. You may choose to turn away from the Real World but it will never turn away from you. You may decide tomorrow to return to the world of broken dreams, but now that you've heard this message you'll not be able to hide as you once did. It's impossible to hide from the Truth forever. You tried and you failed. Let your failure become your greatest success by choosing to end these terrible dreams and enter into the Kingdom whole and wholly loved.

Once again, a resolute, unwavering focus on what is true dispels every illusion. It's a powerful statement that challenges you to let go of your attachment to the illusions that you've created in your mind. It's an invitation to awaken to the truth of who you are and to let go of the false identities that you've adopted.

In order to fully embrace this truth, you must be willing to let go of your attachment to the egoic mind. This means letting go of your attachment to your thoughts, beliefs, and opinions. You must be willing to surrender to the truth and trust that it will guide you to where you need to go.

It can be challenging to maintain this resolute focus in the face of the distractions and temptations of the world. But if you remain steadfast in your commitment to the truth, you'll find that everything else falls naturally into place. Your relationships become more harmonious, your sense of purpose becomes clearer, and your life becomes more fulfilling.

The key to maintaining this focus is to stay present in the moment. Be aware of the thoughts and feelings that arise in you and be willing to let them go. Be willing to let go of the past and the future and be fully present in the here and now.

It's important to remember that your true nature is not defined by your thoughts and emotions. You are not your thoughts; you are the awareness that observes your thoughts. When you remain in this state of awareness, you'll see through the illusions of the egoic mind and embrace the truth of your being.

The illusions of the egoic mind can be powerful, but they're not invincible. When you find the courage to face them head-on and maintain your focus on the truth, you can overcome them. You can let go of your attachments to illusions and embrace the reality of your True Nature.

This resolute focus on the truth is not something that can be achieved overnight. It takes practice and patience. It requires a willingness to let go of your old ways of thinking and being and embrace something new and unknown.

As you begin to embrace this new way of being, you may encounter resistance from others who are attached to their own illusions. You must be willing to stand firm in your commitment to the truth and not be swayed by the opinions of others.

The journey to awakening may not be an easy one, but it is one that's worth taking. As you begin to let go of your attachment to the illusions of the egoic mind and embrace the truth of your being, you'll find that life becomes more joyful, more peaceful, and more fulfilling.

As you move forward on this journey, remember that you are not alone. There is a power within you that is greater than the illusions of the egoic mind. It is a power that will guide you to your True Home, where you're embraced by the love and wholeness you've been seeking all along.

With resolute focus on what is true,
Illusions vanish and dreams are seen through.
The split-mind's dominance begins to fade,
As truth becomes the only thing displayed.

Look not upon the world the split-mind loves,
For every need and want is swiftly solved.
No need to doubt or hesitate in thought,
For dreams have lost their sting and strong onslaught.

The key to unchallenged wholeness now lies,
In holding true to what we realize.
Believe that we are everlasting,
And dreams will fade now with Truth surpassing.

Confusion stems from claims that cannot be,
For they exist outside of God's decree.
Only this truth can stand the test of time,
All else is but a fleeting dream sublime.

You hold the key to open this strong door,
And witness truth sublime never before.
Let go of what is not, embrace the true,
For this is the way to be born anew.

Abandon "Me" to Receive "Thee"

It's clear that we have to completely abandon the lower self in order to reclaim the dominance of the Higher Self. Are there any suggestions you can make that will enable this to occur?

I now open to the Master Teacher within and the Whole Mind that is forever my own.

Everything you need to lift above the restraints of the world you created in your imagination can be found in this statement: I totally abandon "me" to fully receive "thee". This will feel like death until you finally accept that the "me" you've claimed until now is nothing, while the love contained within "thee", or God, is everything. Everything you could ever want or need rests in your acceptance of the Source of all Love, that which created and maintains the entire universe. So don't hesitate. Don't wait for another answer. None will come. Your willingness to abandon your senseless preoccupation with your split-mind and the life you think you live is all you need to receive the Light of God that never fades and could never be extinguished.

The total abandonment of "me" and the complete reception of "thee" is a spiritual concept that emphasizes the importance of laying aside your ego and focusing on the greater good. It involves surrendering your individual desires and goals and instead prioritizing the needs and well-being of others.

At the core of this idea is the belief that the ego is the source of all suffering and that the only path to true happiness is through selflessness. By relinquishing the ego and embracing a spirit of service to others, you can achieve a deeper sense of purpose and fulfillment in life.

In many spiritual traditions, the abandonment of "me" is seen as a necessary step on the path to enlightenment or union with the Divine. By letting go of the small self and embracing a greater reality, you experience a profound sense of connectedness and unity with all things.

While this idea may seem daunting, it's important to note that it's not about sacrificing your well-being for the sake of others. Rather, it's about finding a balance between self-care and service to others, recognizing that your individual happiness is intimately connected to the happiness of those around you.

The abandonment of "me" and the reception of "thee" can take many forms, from small acts of kindness to more significant acts of service. It can involve volunteering, giving to charity, or simply taking the time to listen to and support those around you.

One of the challenges of this concept is that it requires a shift in mindset from a focus on individual achievement to a focus on collective well-being. This can be difficult for those who have been conditioned to prioritize their own success above all else, but it's a necessary step in the journey toward greater spiritual awareness.

Ultimately, the abandonment of "me" and the reception of "thee" is about recognizing that we're all interconnected and that your actions have a ripple effect on the world around you. By embracing a spirit of service and selflessness, you create a more compassionate and just society for all.

This concept is not limited to any particular religion or spiritual tradition but can be found in many different cultures and belief systems. Whether you call it selflessness, compassion, or altruism, the idea remains the same: by putting aside your own desires and needs, you can achieve a greater sense of purpose and connection in life.

In practical terms, the abandonment of "me" and the reception of "thee" may involve letting go of your attachment to material possessions, focusing on the needs of others before your own, and cultivating a sense of empathy and compassion for all beings.

While it may seem challenging to abandon a sense of "me," it's important to remember that this concept is not about self-denial or sacrifice. Rather, it's about recognizing that your true happiness and fulfillment come not from individual achievement, but from your ability to connect with and serve others.

The total abandonment of the personal sense of "me" and the complete reception of the Universal experience of "thee" is a powerful spiritual concept that emphasizes the importance of putting aside the ego and prioritizing the needs and well-being of others. By embracing a spirit of selflessness and service, you can achieve a deeper sense of purpose and fulfillment in life, and create a more compassionate and just society for all.

The "me" within, so selfish and so small
A source of pain, of suffering and strife,
An ego that demands control of all
And blinds us to the beauty of this life.

But in "thee" lies Grace and purest light
A selfless love that radiates and grows,
An open heart that fills the world with sight
And nurtures every blossom as it flows.

To leave the "me" behind and turn to "thee"
Is not to sacrifice or to deny,
But to embrace a path of empathy
And lift our souls to greater heights on high.

For in this act of giving we receive
A sense of purpose, harmony, and peace,
And in the love of others, we believe
That life's true riches do not ever cease.

So let us shed the cloak of selfishness
And find the courage to embrace the light,
To walk with Grace and humble selflessness
And see the world through love's most perfect sight.

For in total abandonment of "me"
And in the total reception of "thee",
We find a joy that sets our spirits free
And fills our hearts with boundless ecstasy.

Only One Choice

The ego believes that it can achieve what it wants by making many, many choices, but I now see that this only distracts us from the single choice that the soul requires to awaken into Oneness. Can you share more about this?

I now open to the Master Teacher within and the Whole Mind that is forever my own.

Does it help you to know that there's only one real choice you can make, the one that matches the choice God makes for you this and every moment? Don't be fooled by the simplicity of that statement; it offers you everything you've been denying yourself. If your choice does not match the choice God makes for you then you deny yourself reception of the eternal experience you deserve. It's always offered but you refuse to receive it, and that's why you're so confused about something that's so simple. Since God is Love and God is ALL that exists, you are wholly contained within the love of God. Accept no compromise to this law. Do you see that every problem you've ever had comes from this compromise?

God's ONE law is unshakable and beyond your ability to change: **only love is real**. In your arrogance, you decided that you can achieve the impossible, but the impossible is what it is because it's not real and never will be. Why are you waiting for a different answer when there is no other voice but the One that speaks for God? None other exists, and this is why salvation is so simple. The only thing that's left is for you to fully accept that which has already accepted you. It is the one thing you have yet to try. Try it NOW!

The simple desire to match God's love for you is all it takes to initiate an avalanche of Grace that overwhelms the illusions you've claimed until now. Does it surprise you that your desire can be such an effective tool? Perhaps you believe that desire is not an attribute of God. How can the "all including Source of universal love" desire anything? And here's your answer: the "all including Source of universal love" desires only to know Itself. In other words, God desires that you know your Self because you are contained within the Source that is God. So set your desire only upon the Source of that universal love and you'll realize that the same Source has forever locked its desire upon you.

The idea that there is only one real choice you can make, the one that matches the choice God makes for you, calls you to align yourself with Divine Will. It suggests that by doing so, you can access the fullness of God's love and the eternal experience it offers. This statement can be viewed as an invitation to let go of your own will and ego-based desires and surrender to the Will of God. By doing so, you can open yourself to receive the blessings and Grace that God offers.

The idea that your choice must match God's choice is a reminder that you're not separate from God, but one with the Divine Wholeness of Reality Itself. By aligning yourself with Divine Will you experience a sense of oneness and unity with God and all of creation. This invitation calls you to let go of any illusions or false beliefs that may be holding you back from experiencing the fullness of God's love. By surrendering to Divine Will you release all limiting beliefs and open yourself to a greater experience of truth and spiritual awakening.

God's ONE law is unshakable and beyond your ability to change. Is that really so hard to accept? It suggests that by aligning yourself with this Truth, you can experience a sense of stability and security in your life. Even someone who has never been exposed to these holy thoughts longs for such stability and security.

The experience that only love is real is the highest that can be reached in this world - a call to let go of fear and embrace a more loving and compassionate way of being. It suggests that by cultivating love in your life, you can experience greater joy, fulfillment, and of course - peace.

What would you lose if you accepted that salvation is so simple? I can tell you what you would gain - literally everything. This may be seen as an invitation to let go of any complicated or confusing beliefs about spirituality and instead focus on the simple truth that God IS love. By embracing this truth, you can experience a sense of freedom and liberation from any belief that still holds you back from this uncompromised and uncompromising experience.

Your thoughts and desires have a powerful impact on your life. By focusing on love and aligning your desires with Divine Will, you can experience a greater sense of peace, joy, and abundance.

God's desire that you know your Self is an invitation to cultivate a deeper sense of self-awareness and self-realization. By embracing this invitation, you experience a greater sense of connection to the Divine and a more meaningful and fulfilling life.

The Source of universal love has locked its desire upon you! Stop and really feel the impact of this. It's a reminder that God's love is always present and available. It suggests that by opening yourself to love, you can experience a greater sense of joy, peace, and purpose in your life.

Never forget, you are wholly contained within the love of God. By embracing this Truth, you can experience a greater sense of self-love and self-acceptance. Where does this lead but to a greater sense of others, then God? All paths lead here.

Every problem you've ever had comes from the compromise you made to the law of love. This call to let go of any negative thoughts or beliefs that may be causing you to suffer is all you need now. By focusing on love and aligning yourself with Divine Will, you can experience a greater sense of freedom and liberation.

Does knowledge serve thee to know there's one choice
That matches the Grace of God's still small voice?
This simple truth offers what you do lack,
Eternal bliss which you choose to turn back.

If thou chooses not what God does command,
Thou'll never receive what thy soul demands,
The love Divine that God's hand now extends,
'Tis the law supreme that thou must not bend.

All woes thou hast arise from this deceit,
The compromise of love thy true defeat.
God's law unshakeable beyond thy reach,
Only true love endures all else doth breach.

In arrogance thou seeketh the unreal,
While love alone remains immutable,
Why seeketh thou answers where none exist,
But the voice of God the source of true bliss.

Salvation is simple in this thy grasp,
Accept that which God hath already clasped,
The one thing left is for thee now to try,
Embrace God's love now and never deny.

A Sufficient Amount of Grace

Why has the secret to enlightenment been so hard to discover? I know it's simple but no matter how high I climb I keep getting pulled back into my ego mind. What advice can you give me to finally help me end this push-and-pull battle?

I now open to the Master Teacher within and the Whole Mind that is forever my own.

We have arrived at one of the greatest secrets for achieving the soul's release into glory. Until now this secret was hidden, and it's important that you realize who set it apart from your Whole Mind. Of course, it was you, the you that you claimed to be apart from the Truth that can never change. You allowed the secret to be hidden because you were determined to deny the simple decision that leads you back to the home you never left. But now a sufficient amount of Grace has entered your mind, and the light accompanying that Grace has illumined the dark corners where you hid from love. This light inspires a desire for even more Grace, and it's this sacred stairway that allows you to match God's eternal love.

Let your desire for love build and your longing increase until there's nothing left in this world for you to seek or allow. God's love for you is eternal and uncompromising, and when you match this uncompromising love you'll wake up in Heaven. Once again, you've claimed that this is what you want, so reach for it now. Let your desire overwhelm all the limiting concepts and illusions that have kept you from the only place you're truly at home.

This is a secret that has been kept hidden for ages, but it's finally time to reveal it. The secret is simple yet profound: surrender. Surrender to Divine Will and allow yourself to be guided by your own Divine Nature. It's only when you let go of your egoic desires and allow the universe to work through you that you can truly be free.

Until now, this secret was hidden, and, yes, it's important that you realize whom it was that set it apart from your whole-mind. It was none other than your own ego, or your identity that kept this secret hidden from you. Your ego thrives on control and will do everything in its power to prevent you from surrendering to Divine Will. But once you become aware of this, you can start to take steps to quiet your ego and allow your soul to shine through.

Of course, it was you, the "you" that you claimed apart from the Truth that could never change, who allowed the secret to be hidden. You were so attached to your identity and your idea of control that you refused to let go and surrender to the Divine. But now is the time to release this attachment and allow yourself to be guided by God.

You're now able to see this clearly and understand that surrendering to Divine Will is the key to your ultimate freedom. The light of Grace has opened your heart and inspired a desire for more - more love, more light, and more truth.

This light inspires a desire for even more Grace, and it's this sacred stairway or ascent that allows you to match God's eternal love. The more you surrender, the more you allow Grace to flow through you, and the more you're able to experience the fullness of God's love. It's a beautiful journey and one that's open to everyone who is willing to let go and surrender.

Let your desire for love build and your longing increase until there's nothing left in this world for you to seek. As you continue to surrender and allow Grace to work through you, your desire for love will grow stronger. You'll begin to realize that the love you seek is already within you and that it's only through surrender that you fully experience it.

God's love for you is eternal and uncompromising, and when you match this uncompromising love, you'll wake up in Heaven. When you surrender completely and allow yourself to be guided by Divine Will, you'll experience a state of pure love and bliss that's beyond anything you can imagine. You'll realize that you're already in Heaven and that it's only your ego that's been preventing you from experiencing it.

Once again, you claim that this is what you want, so reach for it now. You have the power to let go of your ego and surrender to Divine Will. It's only through this surrender that you can experience the fullness of God's love and wake up in Heaven.

Let your desire overwhelm all the limiting concepts and illusions that have kept you from the only place you're truly at home. As you continue to surrender and allow Grace to work through you, you'll begin to see through the illusions and limiting beliefs that have been holding you back. You'll realize that the only place you're truly at home is in the state of pure love and bliss that comes from surrendering to Divine Will.

You've found the key to help your soul's release,
To reach the glory that we long to find.
A secret once hidden now in our peace,
Look within to see who's been so unkind.

The one who kept the truth from your Whole Mind,
It's you, dear self, you denied the embrace,
Of the simple choice, love's decision finds
A home you've never left, a sacred place.

Now, Grace has entered enough to inspire,
A light that shines illuminating all
The darkened corners where we once retired,
And hid from Grace now heeded to love's call.

The light invokes a longing, a desire,
For Grace that leads us to God's sacred love.
The holy stairway, match it and acquire
Uncompromising love, this gift above.

Let love's desire grow, let it increase,
Until there's nothing left for us to seek.
God's love, forever, it will never cease,
And when we match it, it's then we will wake.

In Heaven, our heart has always belonged,
A place that's truly home where we are free.
We've claimed this path, it's what we've always longed,
Now reach for it, let all illusions flee.

The Highest Mountain

Something is shifting and moving inside me. I can feel it deeply like I'm shifting into a whole new way of being. I know these conversations, if that's what I should call them, are a big part of that, but I'd like to understand what's happening with more clarity.

I now open to the Master Teacher within and the Whole Mind that is forever my own.

You're beginning to feel a new level of bright light association coming into your mind. The energy of this is completely different from the world you've experienced before now. It's like climbing the highest mountain on earth. The higher you climb the less oxygen you breathe and the harder it is to perform the simplest tasks, but unlike climbing a mountain, this is the point at which you can release the baggage and the weight of your split identity and claim that which has always been offered by God. At this point you're also beginning to experience the uselessness of the provisions you carried up this mountain. Let them go and you'll fly to the top. Hold on to nothing in this final stage and you'll experience a lightness that transcends this world.

As you embrace this new level of bright light association, you'll find that your mind is becoming clearer and more focused. You'll start to see things with greater clarity and understand the world in a whole new way. The energy of this shift is remarkable, and it's completely different from anything you've ever experienced before.

As you continue to climb this mountain, you'll encounter obstacles and challenges that will test your resolve. But with each step, you'll become stronger, more resilient, and more determined to reach the top. You'll realize that the journey itself is what's truly important and that each step is a step closer to the ultimate goal.

As you reach the higher elevations, you'll begin to experience a sense of detachment from the world around you. You'll start to see that the things that once seemed so important are now meaningless. You'll find that your mind is becoming more peaceful and tranquil, that you're able to experience a deep sense of inner peace and contentment.

At this point, you'll begin to understand the uselessness of the material possessions that you've carried up this mountain. You'll realize that they're nothing more than distractions that keep you from experiencing the true beauty and wonder of the world around you. You find that the things that truly matter are the people you love, the experiences you have, and the moments you share with those around you.

As you let go of the baggage and weight of your split identity, you'll find that your mind is becoming more focused and more aligned with your True Self. You begin to see yourself as a spiritual being rather than just a physical body. You find that you're able to connect with the Divine within yourself and others, that you're able to experience a deep sense of oneness with all of creation.

Continuing to climb higher, you find that the air is becoming thinner and that it's becoming harder to breathe. But despite this, you discover that your spirit is becoming more alive and vibrant. You begin to feel a sense of joy and happiness that you've never experienced before. At this point, it's important to hold on to nothing. Let go of all the attachments that have held you back before now, and allow yourself to experience the true freedom and lightness of being. As you release these attachments you'll be able to soar to the top of the mountain and experience a sense of wonder and awe that's beyond words.

You reach the summit of the mountain and find that there's a whole new world waiting for you. A world of infinite possibilities and endless potential. You find that you're able to see the world in a whole new way and that you're able to experience a deep sense of gratitude and appreciation for all that life has to offer. In this new world, you discover that love is the key to everything. You realize that it's the foundation upon which everything else is built. You also find that as you open yourself up to love you're be able to experience a deep sense of peace and contentment that's beyond measure.

Remember that the journey itself is what's most important. Embrace the challenges and obstacles that come your way and allow yourself to grow and evolve as a spiritual being. As you reach the summit, hold on to nothing and allow yourself to experience the true freedom and lightness of being. Remember that love is the key to everything; it's the foundation upon which everything else is built. Embrace love and allow yourself to experience the wonder and awe of this amazing world we live in.

A new light shines, bright association,
That's sleeping in your mind, a newfound spark.
A different force beyond expectation,
A climb that's like no other in the dark.

Ascending this mountain, higher, higher,
Air grows thin, the weight of self increases.
A struggle that's unyielding like a fire,
Burning now it shakes your soul to pieces.

But at the peak lies something so Divine,
A chance to shed the baggage you once bore.
To leave behind and fully realign,
To God's embrace where love will fill your core.

The provisions you carried now are gone,
A sense of lightness you've never known.
A freedom from the burdens you had on,
A chance to fly and claim your Godly throne.

Let go of all that's holding you behind,
Release the weight and soar up to the top.
Leave all the uselessness in your mind,
Transcend this world, reach for the light, then stop.

A Trick of the Mind

There's still a major belief in separation swimming through my mind, even after this great opening I'm experiencing here. Why is that?

I now open to the Master Teacher within and the Whole Mind that is forever my own.

You believe this world is real because it seems to offer consistent laws that don't change or continuity that can be trusted. But is this really true? Are you ready to consider the possibility that this is a trick that keeps you bound to a world where illusions appear as real and reality is believed to be an illusion? If you are then you're ready to step with confidence into a world where reality is never questioned and the laws of God remain unchanged forever.

There is a parallel between the world you perceive in your so-called awake life and the life you experience when you're asleep and dreaming. You believe that the world you experience when you're awake is real because you wake up in the same bed you went to sleep in, or the relationships you have from one day to the next remain relatively consistent. But it's this relative consistency that needs to be questioned. If you were asleep right now and someone appeared in your dream asking: "how old were you the first time you fell in love," or "where were you living when you were twenty-two years old," you would give an appropriate answer. You would even recall memories from those times and use them as proof that they actually occurred. It's only when you wake up in the morning that you realize that the dream was never real, and the stories you took for reality were fiction.

It's exactly the same when you wake up in the Real World. You realize that the consistent evidence you used to make this world seem real was all in your mind, just as the world you experience in your nighttime dream is all in your mind. Yes, you seem to draw from memories and consistent stories, but at no time are you bound by the laws that make those stories real.

What will you do now that you've heard this put so simply and so clearly? Will you throw up your hands and run out the door, or will you lift your voice in praise to the One who has guaranteed your safety in every imagined reality? The choice is yours, but remember, you will be bound by the choice you make, either Heaven or separation from all that exists. When put so clearly, is there really a choice at all?

As you begin to grasp the possibility that this world is an illusion, you may feel a sense of disorientation or confusion. It's hard to let go of something that seemed so real for so long, and the fear of the unknown may hold you back from taking the leap of faith required to enter the Real World.

However, it's important to remember that the Real World is not truly unknown - it's simply a state of BEING you've yet to fully experience. You are not entering into a void or a blank slate, but rather a world of infinite possibilities and unbounded love. The only thing that's truly unknown in this equation is the ego's fear-based projections of what might happen if you let go of the world you currently perceive.

As you begin to question the reality of this world, you may also start to notice the ways in which it has limited you. Perhaps you've felt trapped or stuck in certain situations, or you've struggled to find meaning or purpose in your life. These limitations are not inherent to your True Self, but rather products of the ego's attempts to create a separate identity.

By letting go of the ego and entering the Real World you can access a state of unlimited possibility and boundless creativity. You're not bound by the laws of the world you currently perceive, but are free to create and express yourself in any way that brings you joy and fulfillment.

As you make the choice to enter the Real World you may also experience a sense of relief or release. The burdens and responsibilities of the world you currently perceive can weigh heavily on you, but in the Real World, you're free to simply BE. You're not bound by the past or the future, but fully present in the eternal Now.

It's important to remember that entering the Real World is not a one-time event, but rather a continuous process of awakening. As you release the ego's grip on your mind you'll begin to experience moments of clarity and peace. These moments are like glimpses into the Real World, and they'll grow more frequent and intense as you continue on the path of awakening.

As you continue on this path, you may also encounter obstacles and challenges. The ego is deeply ingrained in your mind and won't give up its hold without a fight. However, with the help of the Holy Spirit, you can overcome any obstacle and continue on the path of awakening.

Remember that the Real World is not a distant or unattainable goal, but rather a state of being that's always available to you. It's not something that you have to earn or achieve, but a gift that has already been given. All you have to do is accept it.

As you enter into this unified state of consciousness you may also begin noticing a shift in your perception of the world you currently perceive. You'll start to see the world as a reflection of your thoughts and beliefs rather than an objective reality. This shift in perception can be both challenging and liberating as you begin to take responsibility for the world you have created.

Ultimately, the choice to enter the Real World is a choice for love over fear. It's a choice to let go of the ego's illusions and embrace the truth of who you really are. It's a choice to live in a state of infinite possibility and boundless love rather than in a world of limitations and separation.

As you make this choice, remember that you are not alone. The Holy Spirit is always with you, guiding you on the path of awakening and offering you the strength and support you need to overcome any obstacle. With the help of the Holy Spirit, you can enter the Real World and experience the joy and peace that is your natural inheritance.

The world we know it seems so real and true,
With laws that govern all we see and do.
A sense of order, continuity,
That can be trusted, world of unity.

But what if this is just a clever trick,
A subtle game that keeps us bound and sick?
An illusion that appears very real,
A world so fake, where nothing truly heals.

Are you ready to consider and see,
That what you know is not reality,
A world where all is a mere illusion,
And reality a mere confusion?

If you dare step with confidence and trust
Into a world where all is pure and just,
Where the Real is never to be questioned,
And God's law remains forever mentioned.

Then we shall see that all we once believed
Was just a veil that never was achieved.
A sense of peace or an eternal light,
But now we're free and everything is bright.

Denial of Your True Identity

I'm constantly asserting my limited self-identity even though it never gives me what I really want - full release into Oneness. Why does this assertion seem so difficult to break?

I now open to the Master Teacher within and the Whole Mind that is forever my own.

Your self-assertion is the denial of your true reality. There's no possibility that this is not true, and the demonstration of your limitedness is what proves it. As you assert the concepts you've accepted about yourself based upon the unreality of separation, sickness, and death, you seem to become that which you claim. But if that which you claim is not your true identity or your reality, it has no effect. You cannot become something you are not, but this is what you've attempted to do.

All I'm here to tell you is that you failed in your attempt. In fact, you never even came close to success because that which you sought was impossible to gain. In other words, you fell into a state of temporary insanity, and you should be grateful that it was only temporary instead of permanent. It's impossible for you to be permanently insane because it would mean that the assertion of your self-identity has power. It's in reality the definition of powerlessness.

The instant you release the separate or limited self you've claimed until now, you'll be filled with a light so bright and strong that it may seem at first to burn, and indeed this is so. You're burning away that which has never been true, and losing something that has never been true is not true loss. The fire you're feeling is there to burn away the protective armor you used to block the radiance of Heaven's light. So let it penetrate and let it do for you what you cannot do for yourself.

You've wandered into a labyrinth that you cannot escape on your own, but there is One that knows the path to freedom. Surrender to that One and you'll be guided perfectly. Refuse the help that has always been offered and you'll dream of even deeper hells. This is not what you want, but this is what you've claimed by asserting an unreal identity. But the moment of escape has come, and your True Self awaits you at the exit of this pointless labyrinth you've claimed as your home.

Your self-assertion is the root of your suffering. The belief in your limited self creates a constant cycle of seeking and striving, never finding the peace and fulfillment you desire. The more you assert your identity as a separate and limited being, the more you experience the pain and limitations of that identity. The good news is that you can choose to relinquish this false sense of self and awaken to your true identity as a limitless and eternal being. This is the only path to lasting joy and fulfillment.

It may seem difficult to let go of the identity you've claimed for so long, but it's necessary if you want to experience the true freedom and joy that are your birthright. The ego will resist this surrender, but you must be strong and courageous in your desire to awaken. You must be willing to question every belief and thought that reinforces the illusion of separation and limitation. You must be willing to see that you're not a separate entity, but an integral part of the whole of creation.

The moment you let go of your self-assertion you'll experience a profound sense of relief and release. You'll feel the weight of the world lifted from your shoulders and you'll realize that the limitations and struggles you've experienced were never real. You'll begin to see the world in a new light, as a manifestation of the Divine, rather than a collection of separate and disconnected objects and beings.

The awakening to your true identity is not something that can be achieved through effort or striving. It's a Grace that's given when you're ready to receive it. All you can do is prepare yourself by letting go of your false beliefs and opening yourself to the truth. When the moment of awakening comes, you'll know it, and you'll be forever transformed.

You're not alone in this journey. Your Creator is always with you, waiting patiently for you to awaken to your true identity. You have guides and teachers who can help you along the way. You have the wisdom of the ages to draw upon. All you need to do is be willing to take the first step.

The path of awakening is not an easy one, but it is the only path that leads to true freedom and joy. It requires that you let go of everything you thought you knew about yourself and the world, and open yourself to the infinite possibilities of the Divine. But the rewards are worth it. When you awaken to your true identity you'll experience a love and joy that cannot be put into words.

So let go of your self-assertion. Surrender to the Divine. Open yourself to the truth. And let the journey of awakening begin.

Self-assertion denies reality,
Limits seem proven by your strange decree,
Concepts built on the ego's fallacy,
Becoming what could never truly be.

You can't gain what's impossible to seek,
Your attempt at powerlessness so weak,
Temporary insanity so bleak,
Be grateful that the Truth is not so meek.

Release limited self, embrace the light,
At first, it may burn but it's now alight
Burning the falsities, shining so bright,
Heaven's radiance, a beautiful sight.

Escape the labyrinth, surrender to One,
Guided perfectly until freedom's won,
Refuse the help and lose what has begun,
Embrace the True Self, a victory hard-won.

A Million Suns

Even with the demands and restraints of the split-mind, I still feel tremendous bliss building all around me. How can I keep this expanding?

I now open to the Master Teacher within and the Whole Mind that is forever my own.

The bliss you're beginning to feel within explodes like a million suns, yet is as simple and as small as a single flower. When your mind is focused only on the Beloved, you realize that the Beloved is always focused on you. Not the "you" you've claimed but the Self that was claimed before time began. It's this Divine Self that sees only Itself and knows Itself to be the "All in All."

As you surrender your limited sense of self you enter into a state of union with the Beloved. In this state the only thing that exists is pure Love. There are no boundaries, no limitations, and no fear. All that remains is the infinite nature of the Self, and the ecstatic joy that comes with it.

This state of being is not something that can be grasped or held onto, for it is beyond the mind's ability to understand. It's a state of pure awareness where there is no division between subject and object. You realize you are one with everything, for everything is one with you.

In this state there is no need for words for there is only the language of the heart. You communicate with the Beloved through feelings and sensations, and there is a sense of knowing that surpasses all intellectual understanding.

As you continue to surrender more and more you begin to realize that the Beloved has never been separate from you. It's not something outside of yourself that you must strive to attain. The Beloved is already within you, waiting to be discovered.

The journey to this discovery is not one of doing, but of being. It's not about striving for enlightenment or spiritual attainment but about letting go of everything that is not the Beloved. It's a journey of surrender and trust, of letting go of the ego and allowing the Divine to guide you.

As you continue on this journey, you begin to realize that the Divine is not something that can be understood through the mind. It's something that must be felt and experienced in the heart. It's a state of being that is beyond all concepts and beliefs. In this state of union with the Beloved, there is no judgment, no criticism, and no condemnation. There's only unconditional love and acceptance. You're embraced by the Divine and there's a sense of safety and security that's beyond anything you've ever known.

As you continue to surrender the sense of separation begins to dissolve. You realize that you're not separate from the Beloved, but one. You are not a drop in the ocean, but the ocean itself. In this state of union, there is no need for prayer for you now experience constant communion with the Divine. You're immersed in the presence of the Beloved, and there's a sense of awe and wonder that fills your being.

Approaching the end of your journey, you realize that it was never really a journey at all. It was simply a remembering of what you already are. You are the Beloved, and the Beloved is you. There is no separation, no division, and no duality. There is only the infinite nature of the Self and the eternal bliss that comes with it.

As you bask in this state of bliss you realize that it's not something that can be contained or limited. It's something that must be shared with the world. You become a vessel of the Divine, and there's a sense of purpose and meaning that comes with it.

In this state of union, you realize that the only thing that matters is Love. Everything else is an illusion, a dream that has no substance. You are the Beloved, and the Beloved is you. There is nothing else.

Bliss within explodes like a million suns,
Yet small and simple like a single flower,
Focused on this love, realizing runs,
Always focused on you with Divine power.

Surrendering limited self, union,
Pure Love does exist, no boundaries or fear,
Infinite Self, ecstatic reunion,
Grasping impossible, the mind's frontier.

State of pure awareness subjects unite,
Realizing oneness with everything,
Language of the heart, your words not in sight,
Feelings alight, Beloved's offering.

Knowing that surpasses intellect's grip,
State of being, beyond language and lip.

Any Other Goal

All the goals I once had seem to have left me, but if I'm honest I know that there are still some lingering in the back of my mind. Do you have any advice on how these can be finally cleared?

I now open to the Master Teacher within and the Whole Mind that is forever my own.

If there is any goal still left within you other than the attainment of the unified state of being, go and pursue it. You won't achieve Divine Bliss until it's the last morsel left upon your table. If any desire remains within your mind other than achieving the Awareness of Infinite Love, go and seek it. You won't discover the Source that birthed you until you rest content within the Beloved's arms and breathe your last breath.

If there is anything you still desire, need, or long to achieve, then your gaze is still focused outside, the only place your goal will never be found. But when you give up all desire, all need and all longing, the Beloved will appear where she has always been - within the heart of your heart. Seek her there and you'll see your own face radiant and awake.

The Beloved can only be found in emptiness, in silence, where you'll see with the eyes of the One who gave them to you. It is only in this state of complete stillness that you'll find the answers to all of life's deepest mysteries. The Beloved waits patiently for you, never giving up hope that you'll finally return home to the Infinite Love that is your true nature.

When you abandon all other pursuits and devote yourself to the pursuit of the Divine, your life will become like a lotus flower opening to the sun. You'll finally realize that there's no need for anything other than the experience of your true nature. You'll feel complete and content in every moment.

When you've exhausted all other avenues and finally realize that there's nothing left to pursue, you'll discover that the only path left is the path of surrender. Only by giving up all control and letting go of all desires can you find the peace and contentment you seek.

The journey to Self-realization is always a journey of surrender. It's only when you give up the need to control every aspect of your life that you discover the joy of living in the present moment. It's only when you surrender to the Divine that you'll discover your true identity as a child of God.

The journey to Self-realization is not easy, but it is the most rewarding journey you will ever take. I've said this many times and will say it many times more. It requires courage, faith, and the willingness to let go of everything you thought you knew. It requires you to step outside of your comfort zone and explore the unknown.

When you finally surrender to the Divine you'll discover a love that's beyond anything you can imagine. This love will fill your heart and soul and transform your life in ways that you could never have dreamed of. It's a love that's all-encompassing and eternal.

The journey to Self-realization is a journey of the heart. It requires you to let go of all fears and doubts, then open yourself to the love that's within you. It is a journey of self-discovery that will lead you to your true home - the home of the Beloved.

When you finally surrender to the Divine you'll realize that everything in your life has been leading you to this moment. You'll understand that every experience you've had, both good and bad, has been a gift from the Divine, guiding you toward your true purpose in life.

The journey to Self-realization is a journey of awakening. It requires you to wake up from the dream of separation and realize that you're one with the Divine. It's a journey of remembering who you truly are and why you're here.

When you finally surrender to the Divine you'll realize that you've always been loved, even when you thought you were alone. You'll understand that the Divine has been with you every step of the way, guiding you toward your true destiny.

The journey to Self-realization is a journey of love. It requires you to let go of all that is not love and embrace the love that's always within you. It's a journey of discovering the love at the core of your being and sharing it with the world.

When you finally surrender to the Divine you'll understand that love is the key to everything. You'll realize that love is the answer to every question, the solution to every problem, and the way to live a life that's truly meaningful and fulfilling.

If goals beyond the state of Grace do lie,
Pursue them now before your time runs dry.
But know that bliss Divine won't come until
Your table's bare with no desire to fill.

If any craving left within you stays
For love Divine or any other craze,
Go seek it out for until you do so,
You'll never find the source from which you flow.

Your focus on the outside world will lead
To goals that never satisfy your need.
But when you've given up all want and care,
The Beloved will appear, pure and fair.

In emptiness and silence she will dwell,
Where you can see with eyes that know so well.
Only in stillness will the mysteries
Of life be solved, and all its histories.

The Beloved waits for you to return,
To infinite love that's your true concern.
She waits with patience never giving up,
Until you find your way back to her cup.

The Single Goal of the Ego

The ego clearly has a goal in mind, but I'm still confused about what it is. It seems determined to confuse any attempt at singularity and limit its effect. Is there anything specific I should pay attention to that will allow me to be fully open to Oneness?

I now open to the Master Teacher within and the Whole Mind that is forever my own.

The single goal of the ego is to keep your identity in place and give it supreme authority over the world you created in your imagination. What identity do you choose to accomplish this? It doesn't matter as long as its value is unquestioned. The instant it comes under threat it will adapt by seeking a new form to identify with. The ego interprets threat as anything that draws your attention away from its dominance. This could be anything from a deep depression caused by losing someone you love to feeling out of place in a particular body-form identity and choosing another that feels more aligned with "who you really are". You'd be better off admitting that you have no idea who you really are and letting every identifying form fade. Admitting that you don't know who you are is the first step toward being shown the reality of your True Identity which is One with All.

When the ego is threatened, it will do everything in its power to maintain its position of authority over your life. It will manipulate situations and people to protect the identity that it has chosen for you. However, this constant striving to maintain control is exhausting and leads to a life of constant stress and fear.

The ego's fear of losing control is born from the belief that there is something to be gained or lost. The truth is that you already have everything you need within you. You are complete and whole as you are, and the pursuit of external validation and material success will not bring lasting fulfillment.

Letting go of the ego's hold on your life can be scary, as it means facing the unknown and surrendering to a greater power. But when you relinquish control and surrender to the flow of life, you'll discover a deep sense of peace and freedom.

The ego loves to compare itself to others, creating a sense of separation and division. It makes you feel superior or inferior, depending on the circumstance. But in reality, we are all equal and one with the same Divine essence.

When you let go of the ego's grip on your life you'll begin to see the interconnectedness of all things. You'll experience a sense of unity with the world around you, and a deep sense of compassion and love for all beings.

The ego thrives on drama and conflict, as it keeps the mind engaged and distracted from the truth. But when you release the need for drama and conflict you'll experience a new level of inner peace and clarity.

Letting go of the ego is not about denying your individuality or unique expression. It's about embracing your true nature as a spiritual being having a human experience, allowing that essence to shine through in everything you do.

The ego is based on its belief in separation, but in reality, separation is impossible because it is not in the

Mind of God. We're all part of the same Divine consciousness, and when we let go of the ego's illusion of separation we open ourselves up to a world of infinite possibility.

The ego is a construct of the mind, created to protect us from perceived threats. But when we let go of the ego, we realize that there is no real threat, and we can embrace life with an open heart and a sense of wonder and awe.

When we deny the influence of the ego we're not losing anything of value. In fact, we're gaining everything - a sense of inner peace, a deep connection to the world around us, and a knowing that we are part of something greater than ourselves. Letting go of the ego is a journey that requires courage, trust, and a willingness to surrender to the unknown. But when we do we open ourselves to a world of infinite possibility, a deep sense of peace and fulfillment, and a knowing that we're part of something greater than ourselves.

The ego's goal is clear - to keep in place
Your identity with supreme embrace
O'er all the world you've crafted in your mind,
And to its value, you must stay inclined.

The moment that its value comes in doubt,
The ego seeks a new form then to tout.
Threats are interpreted as anything
That challenges its dominance and sting.

Depression, loss, or feeling out of place,
The ego will adapt to save its face.
But true identity is hard to find,
Admitting ignorance can free your mind.

The ego will control with all its might,
Manipulating to stay in the light.
But in this struggle stress and fear abide,
And happiness is hard to find inside.

The Wholeness of God

I would like to hear you share your definition of God. It's clearly the force of this entire conversation but just to be clear, can you break it down for me?

I now open to the Master Teacher within and the Whole Mind that is forever my own.

The Reality you call God is nothing more than the constant, continuous acknowledgment of the wholeness it knows Itself to be. The unreality you call yourself is nothing more than the chaotic assertion of separation you believe yourself to be in relation to the wholeness of God, which you continually deny. Only one of these is true since Reality cannot both affirm and deny Itself. You can choose what you believe to be true, but you cannot make illusions real. This is wholly beyond your ability and the acknowledgment of this would do you well.

The state of humility this acknowledgment inspires is the first step toward being shown a world where illusions never rise to interrupt the Truth. You take it personally when I tell you that the identity you chose, no matter how wonderful it may seem, is in fact an interruption of Truth. The instant you stop taking anything personally you'll realize that you are not a person at all, but the holy perfect child of a wholly perfect Creator.

The ego you have chosen to identify with is the source of all pain and suffering. It is the reason you believe in separation, lack, and limitation. The ego, which is nothing more than a collection of thoughts, beliefs, and emotions, has convinced you that you are separate from the Whole and must fight for your survival. It has convinced you that you are small and powerless, a victim of a hostile world. But in reality, you're one with the Whole, and nothing can harm you or threaten your existence.

The ego is like a cloud that blocks the light of the sun. It obscures the Truth that is always present, never absent. The ego tells you that you must strive to achieve something, that you must become someone, and that you must accumulate things in order to be happy and fulfilled. But the Truth is you are already happy and fulfilled, the only thing you need do is to remove the cloud of ego and let the light shine through.

The Reality you call God is not an external being that you must worship or please. It's the essence of your own being, the source of all life and consciousness. It's the ground of your existence, the substance of your being. It's the infinite, eternal, all-encompassing Presence that pervades everything and everyone. You cannot escape it or avoid it because it is what you are.

The unreality you call yourself is a temporary manifestation of the ego. It's a collection of thoughts, feelings, and sensations that come and go, like waves on the ocean. It has no inherent reality because it's constantly changing and shifting. It's a product of your imagination, a dream that you created and sustain.

The Reality you call God is not a belief or a concept. It's not something that can be grasped or understood by the mind. It's beyond all concepts, beyond all words, beyond all thoughts. It's the pure, unadulterated, unchanging, eternal Presence that is always present, always available, always shining.

The unreality you call yourself is a source of endless conflict and struggle. It's the cause of all pain and suffering because it tells you that you're separate from the Whole and that you must fight for your survival. It tells you that you must compete with others, accumulate things, and protect yourself from harm. But the Reality you call God tells you that you're one with the Whole, that you're loved, and that you're safe and protected.

The ego you've chosen to identify with is the source of all illusions, all delusions, and all misconceptions. It's the veil that covers the Truth and prevents you from seeing it. But the Reality you call God is the light that shines through the veil and reveals the Truth. It's the power that dispels the darkness and brings forth the light.

The unreality you call yourself is a product of time and space, a temporary manifestation of the ego. But the Reality you call God is beyond time and space, beyond all limitations and boundaries. It's the eternal, infinite, all-encompassing Presence that pervades everything and everyone.

The ego you have chosen to identify with is a prison that locks you in a world of fear, lack, and limitation. It's the source of all pain and suffering. But the Reality you call God is the key that unlocks the prison and sets you free. It is the source of all joy, love, and peace.

The unreality you call yourself is like a shadow that disappears when the light shines upon it. It's a mirage that disappears when the Truth is revealed. But the Reality you call God is the Truth that never fades, never changes, and never disappears. It's the constant, continuous acknowledgment of the wholeness.

The Reality of God - endless light,
Acknowledges the wholeness that it knows,
While unreality a simple blight,
Asserts separation - and sorrow sows.

Humility is the first step to Truth,
Illusions never rise to interrupt,
Personal identity is a sleuth,
To hide the perfection bound to erupt.

The ego, a collection of great fear,
Is the source of all pain and suffering,
A dark cloud that obscures the light that's near,
Truth always present, never buffering.

God is not a concept but pure essence,
The ground of all true life and consciousness,
Beyond the mind's words is love's transcendence,
Ever-present, infinite, and endless.

Two Thought Systems

The ego's thought system has never given me what I truly want, though it promises it will. God's thought system, which is love, seems to always give me what I really want - more love. Can you speak more about the differences between these two?

I now open to the Master Teacher within and the Whole Mind that is forever my own.

There are only two thought systems and you demonstrate what you believe to be true through what you teach. But remember, you're only teaching yourself, no matter how deliberate your attempts may be to project another "learner" outside your mind. Teaching and learning are the same in Truth and this is the only thing that concerns us now - the Truth. Your attempts to mix Truth with illusions have failed you over and over, for even when you seem to succeed you've really reinforced the seemingly impenetrable armor you use to deny your own Reality.

Is it strange that the only thing you've mastered until now is denying your own Reality? Admitting this will feel like the greatest possible failure, but your ability to admit that you've done this to yourself is really the first step toward your greatest success.

So what are you waiting for? You feel the stir of this Reality even now as you hear these words. You can listen to them with your ears or your Whole Self. Listening with your ears simply delays your guaranteed return to Wholeness. Listening with your Whole Self establishes the trajectory you need for your final return to Heaven. So once again, what are you waiting for?

The only reason to wait is that you still believe there's something outside of you that you must acquire, attain or accomplish before you can return to your True Self. But this is an illusion and one you've chosen to believe over and over. It's time to let it go and turn within. The True Self you seek is already within you, awaiting your remembrance.

Do not fear the dissolution of the ego-self, for it is nothing more than a mask you've worn to protect yourself from your own perceived separation. When you realize the ego-self is nothing more than a character you've played, a form that you've identified with, you'll be free to relinquish it and discover who you really are.

The path to the Self is not a journey, but a recognition of what has always been true, waiting to be seen. It's not something you must create, but rather it's the very essence of your being. The ego cannot understand this, for it only understands the concept of creation, but the Self is beyond the realm of concepts.

All that's required is your willingness to turn your attention inward, to quiet the mind and allow the Truth to be revealed. The Truth is not something that can be attained through effort or striving, but rather it's revealed when you are in a perfect state of receptivity.

It's important to remember that the journey to Self-discovery is not a linear process, but a spiral. You may find yourself revisiting old patterns and beliefs, but each time you do, you have an opportunity to see them from a new perspective and let them go.

It's natural to feel resistance and fear on this path, for the ego has spent a lifetime identifying with forms and concepts. But each time you choose to turn inward, to listen to the still small voice within, you reinforce your connection to the Truth.

As you move closer to the Truth you may experience moments of deep peace and joy, as well as moments of discomfort and confusion. But know that this is all part of the process and that the discomfort is simply the ego resisting the Truth.

As you continue on this path, you'll come to recognize that the True Self is not separate from anything, but rather the essence of all that is. This realization will bring a profound sense of freedom and a deep sense of interconnectedness.

The path to Self-discovery is not about becoming something you're not; it's about unbecoming everything that you are not. It's a process of shedding the layers of conditioning and false beliefs to reveal the Truth that has always been True.

So if you feel the stir of Truth within you, do not hesitate to turn inward and listen. The journey may not always be easy, but it's the most important journey you'll ever take. And as you come to recognize the Truth of who you are, you'll realize that it has been waiting for you all along.

There are two thought systems you can believe,
Reflected in what you teach and conceive,
Yet know that you are teaching only you,
No matter how deliberate or true.

Two Thought Systems

Teaching and learning merge in Truth alone,
This is the only thing that you must own,
Attempts to mix illusions with the real,
Have failed you time and time again, now feel.

Even when you seem to have great success,
You reinforce your armor, nonetheless,
Deny Reality with all our might,
The only thing you've mastered, that's your plight.

But admitting this is your greatest gain,
And the first step toward ending all the pain,
So why do you still wait to turn within,
When your True Self awaits, free from the din?

Do not fear the ego's dissolution,
It's just a mask to hide the confusion
Of your own unperceived separation
From the Truth of eternal foundation.

The True Self is already deep within,
Awaiting your remembrance to begin.
So listen with your Whole Self and be free,
From illusions blocking Reality.

Total Devotion to God

Many people claim to be convinced of the existence of God, but their lives often don't reflect that claim. What do we need to learn to take the step into total devotion and belief?

I now open to the Master Teacher within and the Whole Mind that is forever my own.

You claim to be convinced of God's existence. If this is true then there is only one course of action left in this world – pursue God with all of your heart, all of your spirit and all of your mind. Anything less than that is hypocrisy. If you claim to be convinced of something so total, be totally devoted to that which you claim to be convinced of.

Words mean nothing to God. Words are invisible to God. Learn this and you will have learned a great secret of the universe. It's the call of the heart that God hears. It's the pounding of love's drum that God responds to. If you claim that God exists but do not give your whole heart to that existence, then you're a fool. A fool claims one thing but does another. All I'm telling you is that if you claim to believe in God, then act like this is so. Otherwise I have no use for you.

To pursue God with all of your heart, spirit and mind requires a complete surrender of the ego. It requires an honest and humble recognition that the ego has no power or value in the pursuit of God. It requires a willingness to let go of all attachments, desires, and beliefs that stand in the way of a direct experience of God's love and presence.

Many people claim to believe in God but are afraid to fully devote themselves to the pursuit of God. They fear the unknown, the loss of control, and the surrender of their own will. They cling to their own beliefs, their own ideas of what God is, and their own limitations. They're not willing to let go of their ego and surrender to the Divine.

But the pursuit of God is not a passive endeavor. It requires action, discipline, and devotion. It requires a daily commitment to prayer, meditation, and service to others. It requires an openness to the guidance of the Holy Spirit and a willingness to follow the path that God sets before you.

To pursue God with all of your heart, spirit and mind is to live in a state of constant surrender. It's to trust in the Divine plan and to allow the Holy Spirit to guide your thoughts and actions. It's to let go of the past and the future and live fully in the present moment, knowing that God is with you always.

The pursuit of God is not a destination, but a journey. It's a journey of the soul, a journey of the heart, and a journey of love. It's a journey that leads to the discovery of your true self and the fulfillment of your deepest purpose.

So if you claim to believe in God, then act like it. Pursue God with all of your heart, spirit and mind. Surrender to the Divine, let go of the ego, and live in the presence of God. The reward is infinite and the journey is the greatest adventure of your life.

If God's existence you claim to believe,
Then one course of action you must achieve.
Pursue God with your whole heart, soul and mind.
Anything less the Truth you will not find.

Words mean nothing, they are invisible,
Learn this secret, it's all divisible,
God hears the call of the heart's loving beat,
To claim belief but not love is deceit.

Many claim belief but fear to pursue,
Afraid of unknown, loss of control too,
To pursue God choose and take strong action,
Devotion, daily prayer, satisfaction.

Trust the Divine plan, surrender your will,
Let the Holy Spirit guide and fulfill,
Live in moment, past and future gone,
Pursue God and forever carry on.

The Kingdom Within the Heart

Jesus spoke about the Kingdom of God and said that it's within each of us. Can you give me advice on how I can find and then express that kingdom in the world I perceive?

I now open to the Master Teacher within and the Whole Mind that is forever my own.

There is a kingdom within the heart that can neither be seen nor understood. Eyes were not made to see such detail and the mind was not designed to understand such grandeur. But the heart itself, the resting place of the kingdom I AM describing, feels that which could never be seen by human eyes, and comprehends that which could never be understood by the human mind.

If you want to know God then seek out the garden where God lives. You'll find the Beloved there, resting beneath the branches of a great willow tree. There's a bench that's only meant for One. Do you see how the Beloved invites you to sit there?

As you approach the willow tree, you feel a sense of peace and tranquility that envelops you. The rustling of the leaves and the gentle breeze is like music to your ears. You sit down on the bench and look around, taking in the beauty of the garden. The flowers are in full bloom, the air is filled with the sweet scent of jasmine, and the grass beneath your feet is soft and green.

As you sit there you become aware of a presence, a sense of love and warmth that fills your heart. You know without a doubt that you're in the presence of the Beloved. You feel a deep connection to this Divine presence, and you realize that you've always been connected to it, even if you were not aware of it.

As you close your eyes and focus on your breath, you feel a sense of peace and stillness wash over you. In this moment, you realize that you're one with the Beloved and that this oneness is the key to true happiness and fulfillment.

You stay in this state of deep meditation for a while, soaking up the energy of the garden and the Beloved. You know that when you leave this place, you'll carry this feeling of oneness with you always, and it will guide you in all your actions.

As you get up from the bench and start to leave the garden, you feel a sense of gratitude in your heart. You know that you'll return to this place often, and that every time you do, you'll be reminded of the love and beauty that exists within you.

You realize that the journey to God is not a difficult one, but rather a simple one. All you need to do is sit in the garden of the heart, and allow the Beloved to reveal Itself to you.

You know that this is not the end of your journey, but rather the beginning. You've taken the first step on a path that will lead you to a state of oneness with all of creation.

As you walk away from the garden, you feel a sense of joy and contentment that fills your entire being. You know that you're on the right path, and that you've finally found the peace and happiness you seek.

You smile to yourself as you realize that the journey to God is not a destination, but rather a never-ending

journey that will bring you closer and closer to the truth
of who you are and will remain for all eternity.

Within the heart lies a kingdom unseen,
Unknown to the mind but felt by the soul.
The Beloved, residing so serene
Within you where peace and harmony roll.

The willow tree sheltering from the heat,
Invites you to sit on a bench Divine.
A presence felt, love and warmth now to greet,
With deep connection eternal and fine.

In this stillness, a oneness is revealed,
A key to happiness the path to God.
A journey not hard but one simply sealed,
In the garden of the heart where we trod.

Leaving the garden we carry within,
Gratitude, joy, and contentment in tow.
The journey not over but does begin,
A never-ending path where truth does flow.

For the journey to God is not a place,
A journey within to love we do race.

True Direction

You speak about whole-mindedness as something that's already true, and the split-mind as an experience that has never been true, though in perception it seems very real. How can I break from this seeming dilemma into a consistent experience of being whole?

I now open to the Master Teacher within and the Whole Mind that is forever my own.

You will know yourself to be whole when you offer yourself "true direction" rather than the split direction you've offered yourself until now. Truth moves in only one direction, not two. Your ego refuses to accept this because its entire thought system is based on the illusion of two, not one.

Trying to reconcile these two opposite views of reality has led you to see a world that's not real. All I'm saying, over and over, is stop trying to reconcile the irreconcilable. Choose to See and you will See. Choose to dream and you will dream. Dreaming an unreal world into existence has led you to believe that your choice of illusions has power. It doesn't. True power comes only when you realize that there's no true choice in reality. There is only One, and what is and remains forever One, is beyond your ability to change.

Recognizing this should bring you great joy because it completely removes the ego's influence. The ego's version of reality is replaced by God's and remains where it has always been. You remain where you have always been as well which is a state of such Grace and holiness that the world of separate forms disappears completely. Why hide from that which your soul longs for? Why deny the only experience that sparks the memory of the Heaven you never really left?

Choosing true direction is the only choice that truly matters because it aligns you with your True Self. When you align with your True Self, you feel the fullness of life and all of its beauty. The split direction you've chosen until now only leads to confusion, doubt, and pain. The split direction, in fact, isn't a true direction at all. It's a direction that keeps you stuck in the illusion of separation.

The only way to move forward in life is to let go of the past and embrace the present moment. The present moment is where you'll find the Truth. It's where you'll find your True Self. It's where you'll find the Kingdom of God. The present moment is where all healing takes place. It's where all transformation occurs.

When you choose True Direction, you begin to live in the world of Spirit. This world is beyond the physical senses. It's a world that's eternal and infinite. It's a world of Love, Light, and Joy. It's a world that is your birthright. It's a world that's waiting to be claimed.

The ego cannot understand True Direction because it's based on the illusion of separation. The ego is a false sense of self created by the mind, separate from others and separate from God. The ego self is not real. It's an illusion that has no power.

The only power that exists is the power of Love. Love is the force that created the universe. It's the force that sustains the universe. It's the force that will bring you back to the Kingdom of God. Love is the force that will transform your life.

Choosing True Direction requires courage and faith. It requires a willingness to let go of the old and embrace the new. It requires a willingness to trust the unknown. It requires a willingness to surrender to the Will of God. When you choose True Direction, you're choosing to live in the Light of Truth.

Living in the Light of Truth means living in a state of Grace. It means living in a state of eternal Joy. It means living in a state of perfect Peace. It means living in a state of consistent Love. When you live in the Light of Truth, you're living in the Kingdom of God.

The Kingdom of God can be understood as a state of consciousness that transcends time and space. It's a state of consciousness that's beyond the physical senses. It's a state of consciousness that's eternal and infinite. It's a state of consciousness that is your true home.

Choosing True Direction is the key to unlocking the door to the Kingdom of God. It's the key to unlocking the door to your True Self. It's the key to unlocking the door to a life of Love, Light, and Joy. The choice is yours. Choose wisely. Choose True Direction.

To know Self as whole you must choose one path,
For Truth moves in a single direction.
Your ego fights this truth clinging to wrath,
And sees a world based on split perception.

Your choice of two views of reality,
Has led you down a path of hurt and pain.
But there's a way to end duality,
And find true peace in the presence again.

True Direction

Choose true direction, align with True Self,
And feel the fullness of life and beauty.
Let go of the past, embrace present wealth,
And step into a world of true duty.

So choose to See, not dream, and you'll be free,
To live beyond the ego's illusion.
It's a world that is eternal you'll see,
As your mind finally receives inclusion.

Remembering Heaven

More than anything, I want to remember Heaven. You say that I never actually left and I'd like to know how to regain that experience.

I now open to the Master Teacher within and the Whole Mind that is forever my own.

When you're unmoved by the strange forms that seem to change and move all around you, you will remember Heaven. You could never completely forget this state of perfect unity because it has never forgotten you. Your true identity may sleep and dream, but the instant you awaken from the dream you'll See everything I'm describing. This could take what appears to be a very, very long time, or it could take an instant. Actually, waking up only takes an instant regardless of your decision. No time can pass in a timeless universe. All is Now, and nothing else exists. This is the experience you deny but once again, it never denies you. Let this realization expand within you, like the branches of a tree providing shade to every creature that stops to rest there.

As you continue on your journey of awakening, you'll begin to notice that the strange forms around you no longer hold any power. They'll appear to change and move, but you'll remain steadfast in your truth. You'll realize that your true identity was never lost or forgotten, but merely sleeping and dreaming. And the moment you awaken from this dream you'll remember everything.

The concept of time is nothing more than an illusion in a timeless universe. Awakening only takes an instant, whether it appears to take a long time or not. All that exists is Now, and nothing else. Once you fully grasp this you'll begin to see everything from a new perspective, one that's filled with clarity, peace, and understanding.

It's easy to deny this experience, but doing so only prolongs the inevitable. When you're ready to let go of the illusions that surround you, you'll find that awakening is not only possible, but it has already occurred. All it takes is a willingness to surrender your old ways of thinking and being, then embrace the truth that has been waiting for you all along.

The truth is always available to you, but you must be willing to seek it out. It may require that you look deep within yourself, and that you confront the parts of you that you've been hiding from. But the reward for doing so is immense, for it will bring you closer to your True Self, and to the Divine that resides within you.

Remember, this journey is not one that you take alone. There are many who have walked this path before you, and there are many who will walk it after you. Seek out those who can guide you and support you, and who can help you to see things from a new perspective. Together, you can create a community of love, support, and understanding.

As you continue on this journey of awakening, know that it is not a destination, but a process. There is no end to the expansion of your consciousness, and there's always more to learn and discover. Embrace this process with open arms, and let the truth guide you every step of the way.

When strange forms move and change all around you,
Stay unmoved and remember what is true.
In perfect unity Heaven awaits,
It never forgets or leaves you to fate.

Your true identity may sleep and dream,
But all dreams must end whatever they seem.
All is Now, though through time you seem to stray,
Eternal rest is yours now and always.

Realize this truth and let it expand,
Like a tree's branches that shelter and stand.
Protecting each creature under its shade,
Holy encounters that will never fade.

On this path of waking soon you will see,
Strange forms no longer hold power, but free,
Be steadfast in your true identity,
No longer lost in strange obscurity.

The Foundation of All Error

The concept of separation had to start somewhere. I'm guessing it began with the idea that Oneness can somehow be separated into parts. Can you speak to me more about that?

I now open to the Master Teacher within and the Whole Mind that is forever my own.

Opposites are reconciled only through Union, joined by the love that created all things as One. The foundation of all error is that the One can become two, or separate into opposing parts. The healing of your split-mind comes naturally when you release such insane concepts, or when you allow Reality to be what it is - REAL. Does this sound simple? It would if you made this decision. What can be more simple than letting Reality be what it is? It's like letting the rain be wet, or the sunshine be warm. There's nothing you need to do for either to be true, but you do need to acknowledge the Truth that is forever True. Once again, this can be simple or complex. As always, it's up to you.

The reconciliation of opposites through Union is a fundamental concept that requires one to acknowledge the interconnectedness of all things. This interconnectedness can be witnessed in the natural world in which all life is dependent on all life. The same concept applies to the spiritual world. When you realize that we are all interconnected, you'll see that separation is an illusion. When you believe that separation is real, you are not living in Truth. The Truth is that we are One, and the power of this Truth is the power that will heal your split-mind.

Healing the split-mind is not an easy task. It requires that you let go of the insane concept that the One can become two, and embrace the Reality that is forever True. This Reality is not complex, it is simple. All you need to do is acknowledge it, and then you'll see that the healing of your split-mind comes naturally. This healing process is like the sunshine warming the earth. It happens without you doing anything.

You are the one who complicate things. You create your own suffering by believing that you're separate from others and the world around you. When you release these insane concepts, you're able to see the Truth that's been there all along. The Truth is that we're not separate, but One. The love that created all things as One is the love that heals your split-mind.

This healing process requires you to be present in the moment. You need to let go of the past and the future and be present in the Now. The Now is where you'll find the Truth. The Truth is not found in the past or the future, it's found in the Now. When you're present in the Now, you're able to let go of the illusions that have caused your split-mind to seem to exist.

Acknowledging the Truth that is forever True requires you to be honest with yourself. You need to be willing to see things as they are, not as you would like them to be. When you're honest with yourself, you're able to see the Truth that's been there all along. The Truth is that we're not separate, but One. The power of this Truth is the power that will heal your split-mind.

The healing of your split-mind requires you to let go of your ego. Your ego is the source of your separation, and it's the source of all your suffering. When you let go of your ego, you're able to see that we're One. The power of this realization is the power that will heal your split-mind.

The power of the Truth will set you free. When you acknowledge the Truth that is forever True, you're able to let go of the illusions that have caused your split-mind. The Truth is that separation is impossible.

Opposites united in Love's embrace
All things as One now connected and whole
Error arises from concepts misplaced
That One can divide and fragment the soul

To heal the split-mind, release the insane
Embrace the Truth that is always revealed
Simple and easy no need now to strain
Acknowledge the Truth that ever appeals.

Wholeness is witnessed in nature's disguise
Life upon life is a delicate dance
Spirit and Grace now reveal the surprise
Separation is a mere happenstance.

The power of Truth, the power to heal
Let go of illusions a vital start
Embrace Reality let it reveal
The healing that comes now from the whole heart.

Sunshine warms the earth, no effort required.
Truth is as real now as rain's soft wet touch.
Acknowledge the Truth, no need for desire.
Opposites reconciled within our clutch.

An Imagined World

You've already said that the mind contains the power of God to create, or miscreate. But miscreation reveals a world of confusion and chaos. Why would we want to choose such an experience?

I now open to the Master Teacher within and the Whole Mind that is forever my own.

The separation you sense in the world is only in your mind, but because your mind is imbued with the energy that created it, you have the power to project what you believe into the world. But you do not have the power to make the impossible real, and separation from Love is impossible. That would mean that the world you think you see is impossible as well. This is the easiest way for you to understand the Truth your Whole Mind knows to be True - the world you seem to see cannot be truly seen, but it can be imagined.

The escape from this way of "not seeing" is simple - choose to See what God Sees instead of what you assert to be real. Then reality itself will collapse time and you'll find your Self where you've always been.

When you choose to See through God's eyes, you choose to see the Love that unites all things. You choose to see the Oneness that exists beneath the illusion of separation. You choose to see the Light that shines within every being, no matter how obscured it may seem. This is True Vision that leads you to the peace and joy that your heart yearns for.

The world you see is a reflection of the thoughts you hold in your mind. It is a projection of the past, an illusion you've created based on your beliefs and judgments. But when you choose to See with God's eyes, you choose to see beyond the illusion, beyond the past, and beyond the limitations of the ego. You choose to See with the eyes of Love, and in so doing, you awaken to the Truth of your Being.

The Truth is that you've never been separated from Love, but are an essential part of it. Love is the foundation of your Being, the essence of who you are. When you choose to See through God's eyes, you remember this Truth, and you allow Love to guide your thoughts, words, and actions.

The world you see is not fixed but is constantly changing based on the thoughts you hold in your mind. When you choose to See through God's eyes, you choose to see the world as it truly is - a reflection of Love rather than chaos. You choose to see the beauty and the wonder that exists in every moment, and in every being.

Choosing to See through God's eyes is not a one-time event, but a continuous practice. It requires vigilance and commitment to Love, and a willingness to release the old patterns and the beliefs that have kept you in the illusion of separation. But the rewards are great - the peace, the joy, and the sense of purpose that comes from living a life aligned with the Truth.

As you choose to See through God's eyes, you'll find that the world around you begins to shift. The people and situations that once seemed threatening or difficult will no longer hold power over you. You'll see them with compassion and understanding, and you'll be guided to respond with Love.

The illusion of separation is not the Truth, but it is a convincing one. It's easy to get caught up in the drama and the chaos of the world and to forget the Truth of your Being. But when you choose to See with God's eyes you remember that you're not separate from Love and that the Real World is a reflection of that Love.

The choice to See with God's eyes is always available to you. You do not have to wait for a special moment or a particular circumstance. You can choose to See with God's eyes right now, in this moment. Simply let go of the thoughts and beliefs that have kept you in the illusion of separation, and allow Love to guide you.

As you choose to See through God's eyes, you'll find that the Love within you is also within others. You'll begin to see the Light that shines within them, and you'll be guided to respond with kindness, compassion, and forgiveness.

The choice to See with God's eyes is the choice to remember the Truth of your Being. It's the choice to remember that you're not separate from Love, but are an essential part of it. It's the choice to live a life that's aligned with Truth and to allow Love to guide you on your journey.

The distance you sense is all in your mind,
Projections of energy that you find.
Thoughts and beliefs that shape the illusion,
Of worlds that seem so full of confusion.

Love is not separate uniting all things,
Oneness beneath all illusions it brings.
See with God's eyes and the Truth will unfold,
Love guides your thoughts, words, and actions so bold.

The world you now see - reflections of mind,
Dreams that now keep you from being aligned.
When Seeing with God's eyes the past dissolves,
The ego's torments no longer involved.

What I Think I Know

I think I know so many things, and I'm certain about what I think I know or understand. But when I really think about it, there's very little that I actually do know. We're constantly learning more, even in our scientific knowledge. Can you speak to me more about that?

I now open to the Master Teacher within and the Whole Mind that is forever my own.

What you think you know is not known by God, therefore it is not knowable. If you share the One Mind that is in God, then anything apart from that Mind is unreal. This is the only lesson you keep resisting. The moment you give up your resistance you'll awaken to the world that's always right in front of you.

This statement also implies that your thoughts and perceptions are not inherently real or true. They're simply mental constructs you use to make sense of the world around you. This can be a challenging idea to accept, especially if you've invested a great deal of time and energy into your personal beliefs and opinions. However, it's essential to recognize that these constructs are not fixed or permanent.

In fact, one of the central teachings of many spiritual traditions is that the true nature of the physical world is impermanent and ever-changing. It's only by letting go of your attachment to your thoughts and perceptions of that world that you can awaken to the deeper reality that exists beyond them all.

When you recognize that you're not separate from this larger consciousness, you begin to see that anything apart from it is, in some sense, unreal. This includes your personal beliefs, your sense of identity, and your attachment to material possessions and worldly success.

This can be a challenging idea to accept, especially in a culture that values individualism and personal achievement. However, it's important to recognize that your attachment to these things is ultimately what causes your suffering and disconnects you from the true nature of reality.

The lesson of giving up your resistance to this truth is a crucial one. It requires letting go of your ego-driven desire for control and embracing the certainty of God.

This can be a scary and unsettling process, as it requires you to confront your deepest fears and insecurities. However, it's also a profoundly liberating experience that allows you to awaken to the true beauty and wonder of the world around you.

When you let go of your resistance to the One mind that is in God you begin to see that the world you've been searching for has been in front of you all along. You realize that Heaven is not some far-off destination or otherworldly realm but a state of being that's available to you in the present moment.

In the end, the lesson is a simple one: let go of what you think you know, embrace the mystery and wonder of existence, and awaken to the truth of the One Mind that is in God. It's only by surrendering to this truth that you discover the true nature of your being and experience the profound peace and joy that comes with it.

The knowledge you believe to be so sure,
Is not known by One who reigns from above.
Only Divinity can know what's pure,
Anything else is not real but a bluff.

This lesson you keep resisting in vain,
For the truth is what you need to attain,
And the moment you give in to its call,
You'll finally know Heaven awaits us all.

This world is a dream that you now create,
And in your mind, it seems to be so real,
But all is illusion that you must negate,
To see the truth that lies beneath the veil.

Let go of resistance, give up the fight,
Let God's perfect Love guide you to the sight
Of a world forgiven in front of you,
The Heaven you never left, always true.

The Fuel for Freedom

What's the most important thing we need to break free from the ego's domination?

I now open to the Master Teacher within and the Whole Mind that is forever my own.

Just as a rocket ship needs enormous energy to break free from the gravitational pull of the earth, so do you need enormous passion and love to break free from the gravitational pull of the ego. Your desire for Oneness is the fuel and yet without a guidance system the ship would spin through the emptiness of space and never reach its destination. An astronaut must learn to trust the ship's guidance and let it do its job, which it does perfectly. And you must learn to trust the Holy Spirit which is your guidance system. There is no confusion there, while confusion is still very much present within your mind. Trust the ONE who knows, then you'll realize that YOU have always been Known. Then you'll arrive safely at the predetermined location, the Heaven where you are at Home.

It seems that breaking free from the gravitational pull of the ego is an impossible task. What if I told you that it's already been accomplished and all you are doing is remembering something that is true NOW? The Truth of you is True NOW. The Reality of you is Real NOW. You're being asked to accept what has always accepted you, for if you do you'll experience something that transcends the world you've claimed until now, and step into the Real World where love is not opposed. In this world there is no need for you to be healed.

To fully experience this Real World you must release any attachment to the illusions of the ego. This means recognizing the false narratives and stories you've created for yourself and letting them go. Only in this way can you step into the truth of who you are and experience the freedom that comes with it. This freedom allows you to express your Authentic Self in every moment, without fear or reservation.

The ego operates on a constant cycle of seeking and needing, which can never truly be fulfilled. It's only when you relinquish this cycle that you can fully embrace the wholeness and completeness that is your natural state of being. It's a letting go of the illusion of lack and embracing the abundance that's always available to you.

This abundance is not just material, but it's a deep sense of inner peace, joy, and love that comes from knowing that you're connected to something greater than yourself. This connection is to the Divine, the Universe, the Source of all that is. It's the recognition that you're an integral part of this Oneness, and that separation is an illusion created by the ego.

As you continue to let go of the ego, you'll find that your life becomes simpler, more effortless, and filled with more joy and peace. You'll begin to experience life as a flow, rather than a struggle. This is because you're no longer fighting against the current of life, but instead, you're allowing it to carry you forward.

It's important to remember that this journey is not about reaching a final destination, but about experiencing the journey itself. Every moment is an opportunity to deepen your connection with the Divine, and to experience the beauty and wonder of life. Each step is a reminder that you are loved and supported by a power greater than yourself.

Ultimately, the goal is not to transcend the ego, but rather to integrate it into a larger understanding of who you really are. It's about recognizing that the ego is a tool to be used in service of the Higher Self, rather than something to be feared or rejected. When used in this way, the ego can become a powerful ally in your journey of self-discovery and growth.

Breaking free from the gravitational pull of the ego requires passion, love, and a deep desire for Oneness. It's not an impossible task, but one that requires trust in the guidance of the Holy Spirit and a willingness to let go of the illusions of the ego. Through this process, you can step into the Real World where love is not opposed, and experience the abundance, joy, and peace that is your natural state of being.

Passion and love are the fuel for your flight,
Guidance above is your beacon of light.

With passion and love, you've set on a quest,
To break free from ego's unyielding grip.
But just as a rocket needs guidance to crest,
Your course needs a system to guide this ship.

Passion and love are the fuel for your flight,
Guidance above is your beacon of light.

The fuel for your journey - Oneness desired,
But without true guidance - spin into space.
Your path must be clear, not muddled or mired,
For your destination now is God's Grace.

Passion and love are the fuel for your flight,
Guidance above is your beacon of light.

The journey is long but you will arrive,
In Heaven where you have always belonged.
With the Holy Spirit, you then will thrive,
And discover that you're forever known.

Passion and love are the fuel for your flight,
Guidance above is your beacon of light.

Perfect Non-Being

Anyone who has ever glimpsed the experience of wholeness or enlightenment knows that it's the only thing the soul longs for. So why do we tend to perceive the release from the split-mind or ego as something to be afraid of and avoid?

I now open to the Master Teacher within and the Whole Mind that is forever my own.

You are being called into a state of Perfect non-Being, which until now you've interpreted as death or loss. Perfect non-Being is actually the dissolving of the separate-self and the rising, or resurrection, of your Sacred Self. When the Sacred Self rises it is transformed and is no longer bound by the same laws that once seemed so insurmountable. This is the transcendent reality we share, regardless of you being aware or unaware of what is real. Much like gravity, you don't need to acknowledge its power to feel gravity's affect.

It's important to note that the ego is not inherently bad or evil, but it can create a sense of separation and limit your experience of the infinite possibilities of the universe. By releasing your attachment to the ego, you open yourself to a deeper connection with your true nature, which is boundless and infinite.

Many spiritual traditions teach that the ego is the source of suffering, and that the ultimate goal of spiritual practice is to transcend the ego and find liberation. This can be a challenging journey, but it's ultimately worth it, as you discover the truth of who you are and experience a deeper sense of purpose and fulfillment in life.

One of the keys to transcending the ego is to cultivate a daily practice of meditation or mindfulness, which can help you become more aware of your thoughts and emotions, and develop a sense of detachment from them. This detachment can allow you to see your thoughts and emotions more objectively, and not be so caught up in the drama and chaos of your daily life.

Another important aspect of transcending the ego is to cultivate a sense of compassion and empathy for others. When you see beyond your own self-centered concerns and truly connect with others on a deep level, you begin to dissolve the boundaries that separate you and tap into the universal love and wisdom that permeates all of existence.

Ultimately, the journey of transcending the ego requires a deep commitment to spiritual practice, as well as a willingness to face your fears and limitations head-on. But when you're able to break free from the gravitational pull of the ego and connect with your true nature, you discover a sense of peace, joy, and fulfillment that is beyond anything you could have imagined.

As you are called to states of non-being,
The ego's grip must loosen its tight hold.
To rise again your Sacred Self freeing,
And watch as its true form does now unfold.

Release now your grasp on what's never True,
Boundless and infinite at last in view.

Once thought of as a loss or death to mourn,
Perfect non-being is the way to rise,
To shed the limits once thought to adorn,
And transcend beyond all these earthly skies.

Release now your grasp on what's never True,
Boundless and infinite at last in view.

The ego's power, not inherently bad,
But separation it can now create,
To limit experiences we've had,
And obstruct all our connections and fate.

Release now your grasp on what's never True,
Boundless and infinite at last in view.

Be Present to the Presence

It sounds so simple when you explain it, but in practice, it sometimes feels so far away. Can you speak more about Perfect non-Being?

I now open to the Master Teacher within and the Whole Mind that is forever my own.

To realize the state of "Perfect non-Being" simply relax and be present to the Presence of I AM. A river flows without effort toward the ocean just as you flow effortlessly toward the ocean of Infinite Being. If you surrender to the current you'll realize that though the quality of the river and the ocean differ, they're actually connected and one. You'll also realize that when the river reaches the ocean the river's current is no longer required. What is the purpose of the river's current? It is to draw you to the ocean. Once you arrive, your Being expands to include not only the river but every river that empties into the ocean. It is this emptying that's important. Let the current take you, then empty yourself of every longing and desire but to be one with this Infinite Ocean of Grace. Think of nothing but this, then you'll dissolve and know that the river and the ocean are one.

As you journey toward the state of Perfect non-Being, it's important to remember that this state is not something that you can achieve through effort or willpower. It's a state of Grace that arises naturally when you let go of the need to control your experience and simply allow yourself to be present to the present moment.

One of the key components of this journey is to develop a deep sense of trust in the process of life. Trust that you're being guided and supported every step of the way and that everything that's happening in your life is happening for your highest good.

Another important aspect of the journey toward Perfect non-Being is to develop a sense of detachment from the outcomes of your actions. Instead of being attached to specific outcomes, simply do what you feel called to do in each moment and trust that everything will work out as it should.

As you continue on this journey, you may find that you encounter obstacles and challenges along the way. These obstacles are simply opportunities for growth and learning and can be embraced with a sense of curiosity and wonder.

In addition to cultivating a sense of trust and detachment, it's also important to cultivate a sense of gratitude and appreciation for all that life has to offer. When you're able to see the beauty and wonder in even the most mundane aspects of your lives, you open yourself up to a deeper sense of connection with the universe and all beings.

Another important aspect of the journey toward Perfect non-Being is to develop a sense of compassion and empathy for yourself and others. When you can see beyond your own self-centered concerns and truly connect with others on a deep level, you begin to dissolve the boundaries that separate us and tap into the universal love and wisdom that permeates all of existence.

Ultimately, the journey toward Perfect non-Being is a journey toward greater self-awareness and self-realization. It requires a deep commitment to spiritual practice, as well as a willingness to face your fears and limitations head-on. But when you're able to break free from the gravitational pull of the ego and connect with your True Nature, you discover a sense of peace, joy, and fulfillment that is beyond anything you could have imagined.

In this state of Perfect non-Being, you're able to see beyond the limitations of your individual self and connect with the infinite potential of the universe. You're able to tap into the creative power of the universe and bring forth your own unique gifts and talents in service to the world.

So as you continue on your journey toward Perfect non-Being, remember to stay present to the present moment, cultivate a deep sense of trust and detachment, and embrace the obstacles and challenges that arise with a sense of curiosity and wonder. And above all, remember to be kind, compassionate, and loving toward yourself and all beings, as we're all connected in the infinite ocean of Grace.

Relax and be present to I AM's touch,
Like rivers flowing desiring so much.
Surrendering to the current and flow,
Toward Infinite Being's eternal glow.

The river and ocean may seem apart,
Yet they are connected in one great heart,
When the river meets the ocean's embrace,
Its current's purpose is fulfilled with Grace.

Let yourself empty, be free of desire,
Be one with the infinite and aspire,
Dissolve in the ocean's boundless expanse,
And know the river and ocean's true dance.

This holy state of Perfect non-Being,
Your Sacred Self in true form is freeing,
Your being expands to every true source,
Infinite blessings your nature endorse.

Teacher of God

How would you define who I am at the most fundamental level?

I now open to the Master Teacher within and the Whole Mind that is forever my own.

You are a Teacher of God because it's impossible for you to be anything else. This fact will fill you with either great happiness or tremendous fear, depending upon how willing you are to release the perceptual chains you've wrapped around yourself. Does it help to know that the chains are not real? They have no weight and possess no power, but because your mind has given them great power they seem to be heavy and impenetrable. A Whole Mind is simply One that has shaken these imaginary shackles from their ankles and realized their non-reality.

Once again, you are a Teacher of God but until now you've refused to teach God's curriculum, a choice that brought you intense despair. God's curriculum is always love but you've been teaching that there's an alternative to love. This seeming alternative has built an unreal façade that seems from one angle to be real, just as a movie set seems real until you walk through the door and realize that there's nothing of real substance there.

The Holy Spirit is calling you to teach what is True, not illusory. God is calling you away from unreality into the Real. The only question now is how long will it take for you to answer that call? Perhaps it helps you to know that the choice has already been made. You answered the call the instant it was offered, but you also found a way to stretch out time and make it seem like a distant goal. Accept salvation now and you'll realize that it is NOW.

There's no reason to delay your recognition of what has always been True.

As a Teacher of God, you have a unique responsibility to offer guidance to those who are willing to learn. However, you cannot fulfill this role until you first teach yourself the Truth - that Love is the only reality. This means releasing all attachments to the ego's false thought system and aligning with the Holy Spirit's curriculum.

It's important to remember that you're not the source of the teachings you offer. You're merely a conduit for the messages of love that flow through you. Your job is to simply be open and willing to allow the Holy Spirit to work through you.

As you teach God's curriculum, you'll begin to see the world in a whole new light. What once seemed dark and chaotic will be transformed into a radiant expression of Love. This is not a fanciful dream, but a direct experience of the Truth.

The more you teach God's curriculum, the more you'll realize that it's the only thing worth teaching. Everything else is just a distraction that leads to pain and suffering. You'll be filled with a deep sense of purpose and joy as you offer the light of Truth to those around you.

As a Teacher of God, you must be willing to let go of all judgment and condemnation. You must be a living example of the love and acceptance that you're teaching. This means you must be vigilant in your thoughts and actions, always looking for ways to extend the love that you have received.

The world needs more Teachers of God. The darkness and fear that seem so pervasive are nothing more than illusions. As you teach Love, you become a beacon of hope in a world that's desperate for the Truth.

The power of a Teacher of God is not found in their credentials or their status. It's found in their willingness to surrender to the Love that flows through them. This is the only real power there is, and it's available to all who are willing to receive it.

You don't need to be a master or a saint to be a Teacher of God. You only need to be willing to learn and share the lessons you've learned. The Holy Spirit will guide you every step of the way, so there's no need to worry about making mistakes.

The role of a Teacher of God is not a burden, but a blessing. It's an opportunity to give and receive the Love that's our natural inheritance. It's the chance to help others remember who they truly are and to awaken to their own Divinity.

As you teach God's curriculum, you'll come to see that there's nothing more important than the Truth. All other concerns fade away in the light of this realization. You'll find a peace and joy that cannot be found in the world.

The call to be a Teacher of God is a call to return Home. It's a call to remember your Oneness with God and to share that remembrance with others. It's a call to be a miracle worker, to bring healing and transformation to a world that sorely needs it.

So answer the call, dear Teacher of God. The world is waiting for you.

You are God's Teacher and this you must know,
I promise it's true and always is so.
This true fact may bring you joy or great fear,
Depending on your desire to be clear.

The chains that bind your mind in perceptions,
Illusions that have gained false conceptions.
But let it be known, these chains are not real,
No weight or power they only conceal.

A Whole Mind is one freed of such shackles,
Lifting instead to great tabernacles.
God's curriculum is Love, you will see,
Ego's alternative never will be.

A choice that brings despair and misery,
A façade built up - false reality.
Yet, you are a Teacher of God, no less,
And teaching Love will free you from distress.

The Greatest Confusion

At first glance this is all so confusing, but the deeper I go into the experience, the clearer the Truth becomes. It seems that confusion is one of the ego's primary tools. Is this correct?

I now open to the Master Teacher within and the Whole Mind that is forever my own.

It's clear that the split-mind or split-self intends to confuse your Real-Self because this is how it maintains its illusory dominance over your life and everything you perceive. But the ego also confuses itself in its constant preoccupation with making the real seem unreal, or the truth untrue. In other words, The ego is so completely confused that it confuses even itself.

If you're able to look at this honestly, it will explain nearly everything you seem to be confused about. Confusion begets more confusion but the truth makes everything clear. If you're confused about anything, especially your own identity, it means you're distracted by the ego's need to confuse itself. Be distracted no more! Listen only to the Voice for God that speaks within you. It's not confused at all and looks upon your reality as it looks upon Itself. How could it look upon you in any other way since it knows you to be One with all that It is?

The egoic thought system is founded upon the belief that separation is possible and necessary. It's as though the ego exists simply to make this one point - that the One can become two, and two can become many. The ego maintains this illusion by using confusion as its primary tool. It makes the real seem unreal and the truth seem untrue. This confusion has become so deeply ingrained in your mind that you usually don't even know that you're confused.

But there's a way out of this confusion, and it's by recognizing that it's not real. You can choose to stop believing in the ego's illusions, which have no foundation in Truth. Instead, listen to the Voice for God that speaks within you. This Voice is always clear and never confused, and it sees you and everything else as Itself.

The ego's confusion stems from its belief that it's separate from everything else, including God. This belief creates a sense of lack and fear, which drives the ego to constantly seek validation and control. But the truth is that you are One with God and all that exists. When you recognize this truth, the ego's confusion fades away, and you can see clearly.

When you're confused, it's easy to feel overwhelmed and powerless. But you're not powerless, and you're not alone. The Voice for God is always with you, guiding you toward Truth. You can trust this Voice completely because it's the Voice of Love, which is always gentle and kind. It will never lead you astray, and it will never leave you lost and confused.

As you begin to let go of the ego's confusion, you'll find that you feel lighter and more peaceful. You'll be able to see the world with new eyes, and you'll understand that everything is a reflection of your own mind. The confusion that once seemed so pervasive will start to fade away, and you'll experience a deep sense of clarity and understanding.

Confusion is not your natural state, and it's not necessary for you to live a fulfilling life. When you allow the Voice for God to guide you, you'll experience a deep sense of purpose and meaning. You'll know that you're loved and supported and that you have everything you need to live a joyful and abundant life.

The ego's confusion is like a veil that covers your eyes, making it difficult to see the Truth. But this veil is not real, and it can be lifted at any time. You don't have to wait for some future moment to experience clarity and understanding. You can choose to let go of the ego's confusion right now and step into the light of Truth.

The more you practice listening to the Voice for God, the more you'll recognize the ego's confusion for what it is - a meaningless distraction from the Truth. You'll see that the ego's illusions have no power over you and that you're free to choose a different way of seeing.

The confusion you feel is simply a symptom of the ego's belief in separation. When you recognize that you're One with all that exists, confusion fades away, and you experience the peace and joy that are your natural state. So, if you find yourself feeling confused, remember that the confusion is not real and that you can choose to instantly let it go. Listen to the Voice for God, and trust that it will guide you toward the clarity and understanding that you seek.

The split-self seeks to confuse and deceive,
And keep you bound in its illusory weave.
In its confusion it deceives as well,
Creating unskilled its own perfect hell.

The ego's game is to hold and confuse,
But the Voice for God will never refuse.
Surrender it all and all you will Know,
Heaven will answer the call of your soul.

Listen to God's Voice, it will guide your way,
God sees you as One with all, day by day.
God only views you in this sacred light,
For you are part of God's infinite might.

No longer distracted confusion goes,
Let the Voice for God within you now grow.
Its clarity will guide you to the end,
And reveal the Oneness you now transcend.

The Escape Hatch

Is there a way to speed up the process of awakening or find a path that leads directly to Whole-Mindedness? I guess I'm asking if there's an escape hatch we can open and move out of the ego-mind directly into the Real World.

I now open to the Master Teacher within and the Whole Mind that is forever my own.

You dream of impossible worlds where you have the power to make the unreal real, but at no time is this actually true. This, by the way, is your salvation, the escape hatch that releases you from the world of sickness, pain, and death. You've been sold the idea that in order for you to BE, sickness, pain, and death are inevitable. And so they are, but only because you believe they are. What do you think would happen if you had a direct experience of the True Reality of your BEING, which is eternal, whole, and invulnerable? Is it possible that the world you created in your imagination would remain? Or would it dissolve in the brightness of your discovery?

A Whole Mind is simply one that declares and affirms the Reality that is forever Real while ignoring the illusions that were never real. This isn't a mental declaration or intellectual decision. It may begin through the assertion of the reasonableness of eternal Oneness, but the escape hatch into the Real World doesn't happen through the mind but through the passionate release of the intellectual mind and all its constricted ways. Imagine you've been wearing a heavy, tight suit of armor your entire life, then imagine the freedom you would feel when it falls off your body to the ground. This is only a hint of the release you'll experience when your perceptual mind fades, replaced by the Wholeness that has never been compromised.

It may be difficult to believe that the world you see is an illusion, especially when you've invested so much time and energy into it. But the world you think you see is only a projection of your mind, and it can change in an instant when you shift your focus to the Reality that is forever Real. The key to this shift is to recognize that your imagination has no power over Reality and that the illusions you've created can be released when you're ready to let them go.

When you declare and affirm the Reality of your BEING, you begin to let go of the illusions that have kept you bound to the world of sickness, pain, and death. This declaration isn't something you can think your way into, but something you must experience on a deep level. It requires that you release the constrictions of your intellectual mind and open yourself to the Wholeness that has never been compromised.

The path to Wholeness requires that you be willing to release the chains of perception that have held you captive for so long. This may be scary at first, but it's the only way to experience the True Reality of your BEING. You must be willing to look honestly at your confusion and recognize that it's simply the ego's attempt to confuse you further. When you stop listening to the ego's voice and start listening to the Voice for God, you begin to experience the clarity and peace that comes with knowing the Truth.

It's important to remember that your imagination is not real and has no power over Reality. You can dream up all sorts of impossible worlds, but they'll never be real. Your salvation lies in recognizing this and shifting your focus to the eternal, whole, and invulnerable Reality of your BEING. When you do this, the world you created in your imagination will dissolve in the brightness of your discovery.

Once again, the escape hatch into the Real World doesn't happen through the mind but through the passionate release of the intellectual mind and all its constricted ways. It requires that you let go of your need to control, then surrender to the Reality that's forever Real. This surrender may be scary at first, but it's the only way to experience the freedom and Wholeness that you seek.

A Whole Mind is simply One that has shaken off the chains of perception and recognized the non-reality of the illusions that once held you captive. This ONE has declared and affirmed the Reality of your BEING and has let go of the ego's need to confuse and confound. You've opened yourself to the Voice for God and have experienced the clarity and peace that comes with knowing the Truth.

It's up to you to choose whether you want to remain bound by the world of illusions or break free to experience the Reality of your BEING. The choice is always yours, and it's never too late to make it. You can start right now, in this moment, by declaring and affirming the Reality that is forever Real and by letting go of the illusions that have kept you bound for so long.

When you do this, you'll experience the freedom and Wholeness that has been waiting for you all along.

In dreams you wield a power all your own,
Creating worlds impossible and grand,
A distraction from the world you have known,
Where sickness, pain, and death hold tight your hand.

This strange escape is but a fleeting thrill,
A product of mind's imagination,
For in the Real World, none of this is real,
A mere illusion in your perception.

And if you were to see Reality,
The True Being that is forever whole,
Would all your dreams remain or simply flee,
Dissolving in the brightness of your soul?

To affirm this Reality is key,
Declare it as forever true and real,
And let the mind's constraints and limits free,
For only then to you the truth reveal.

Imagine shedding armor heavy, tight,
The freedom and release you would then feel,
This is the freedom from perceptual sight,
And the Wholeness that all your wounds would heal.

A Temporary Diversion from the Inevitable

I understand that the Truth is within me and within everyone, but for some of us the experience of that Truth seems isolated and far away. I know the Truth and I want to live within that knowing. Can you help me get closer to that experience?

I now open to the Master Teacher within and the Whole Mind that is forever my own.

You cannot unknow what you already know, but you can ignore or block what you know. You already know that you're whole and protected within the Mind of God. You already know that you've been blessed by the Divine Breath of God. You've hidden from this but it's impossible for you to escape from it.

That's what I mean when I say that you cannot unknow what you know to be true. The Truth has nothing to do with your belief in the Truth. It exists wholly and completely independent of your belief. But it does not exist independent of your experience, and that's why it's impossible for you to escape reality. You can hide for what seems to be a very, very long time, but in the end it's guaranteed. All you need to do is to relax and let the current of this mighty river pull you effortlessly to the infinite ocean you sometimes call God. There's no time in which the river and the ocean are separate, so why would you hesitate?

Once you let go of your resistance, you'll realize that you've been carried all along. Resistance is nothing but a temporary diversion from the inevitable, the recognition of the Reality of your Being. Your resistance stems from a false sense of control, a misguided belief that you're in charge of your own destiny, but in truth, you're not in control of anything. The Truth is already present within you and it's simply a matter of surrendering to it.

As you surrender, you'll begin to see that the ego's perception of the world was nothing but a strange dream, a fleeting experience that had no lasting reality. You'll discover that the only Reality is the Eternal Presence that's always here, always now. This realization is not something to be gained but rather, to be remembered. You're not creating this reality, you're simply becoming aware of what has always been there.

Once you've remembered the Truth, the illusions you have held onto for so long will begin to dissolve. You'll start to see that all the things you once feared and struggled against were never real, and that they never had any power over you. You'll begin to see that you're not a helpless victim of circumstance, but rather, a powerful co-creator of your own reality.

This new perspective will allow you to live in the world with a newfound sense of peace and freedom. You'll no longer be weighed down by the burdens of the past or the fears of the future, but will instead live fully in the present moment. You'll be able to see the beauty and wonder of the world around you, and will begin to experience life in a whole new way.

The shift in your perception will not only change the way you see yourself and the world, but also the way you interact with others. You'll begin to see everyone as part of the same whole, and will treat them with the same love and respect that you would give to yourself. You'll begin to recognize that the separation you once believed in is an illusion and that all beings are connected as One.

As you continue to live from this new perspective you'll find that your life becomes richer, fuller, and more fulfilling than you ever thought possible. You'll begin to see the world with the eyes of a child, curious and open to all that life has to offer. You'll become a Teacher of God, sharing your light and your love with everyone you meet, and inspiring them to remember the Truth that lies within them as well.

Let go of your resistance, surrender to the Reality of your Being, and allow the current of the river to carry you effortlessly to the ocean of infinite love and peace. The journey may seem long and arduous at times, but the destination is guaranteed. So why would you hesitate? The Truth is waiting for you, and it's more beautiful and more wonderful than you could ever imagine.

Inevitable Truth cannot ignore,
Nor block what you already came to know,
Protected by the Divine you are whole,
And blessed by God's breath it's now time to show.

Though hidden it's impossible to flee,
The reality you cannot escape,
What's true, you cannot unknow or unsee,
Believe or not Truth exists in its shape.

The experience or true evidence,
The Truth now impossible to evade,
Hide if you want but in the end immense,
Relax in the current, don't be afraid.

Effortlessly the river will now take,
To the infinite ocean that's your call,
Don't hesitate, there is no time to make,
The river and the ocean, one and all.

Take Nothing Personally

I find myself taking what other people think of me personally. But I also know that in Truth I'm not a person at all - I AM Soul. What advice can you give that will help me let go of other people's judgments?

I now open to the Master Teacher within and the Whole Mind that is forever my own.

Taking anything personally requires a misidentification of your reality. When you realize you're not a person, subject to all the limiting beliefs you've embraced as a person, any opinion anyone has about you will feel meaningless. You won't react, just as you wouldn't react to someone having an opinion or a judgment about someone you've never met. The fact is, you've never actually met the one you've identified as yourself because the one you've identified as yourself isn't real. If you could relax into that fact you would instantly wake up in Heaven.

Realize this and you'll be free from the constraints of limited, split-identity. The wholeness and totality of your True Self will alight in your mind and you'll instantly forgive anyone who misidentifies that which you have fully identified as the perfect extension of love. And of course, this does not stop with you. There is no actual "you" just as there is no actual "other". Only love is real, which is the same as saying that only God exists.

God takes nothing personally because there is nothing outside of God to judge God. All things are unified within the Mind of God and nothing has ever separated from that Mind. You've chosen to live within an illusion where separation seems possible, but at no time did anything separate from the inseparable. The concept of "other" or "personal identity" dissolves in the brightness of this Light. You realize you are the very Light you seek, not a separate person who takes anything personally.

Don't take anything personally and make no one a person. This is the only thing I'm here to teach you.

It can be difficult to let go of your identification with your ego and the idea of a separate self. You often feel like your opinions, beliefs, and experiences define who you are as a person. However, when you realize that your True Self is not defined by these things, you can begin to detach from the need to take anything personal. You begin to see yourself as part of a greater whole, rather than a separate individual. This leads to a greater sense of peace and connectedness.

When you take things personally, you're essentially saying that someone else has the power to define who you are. You're allowing your opinions and judgments to shape your reality. But when you realize that you're not defined by these external factors, you can begin to reclaim your power. You can begin to see that the only person who has the power to define you is you.

One of the keys to not taking things personally is to develop a deep sense of self-awareness. This means becoming aware of your thoughts, feelings, and reactions in the moment. By being present and aware, you can begin to notice when you're starting to take things personally and begin to detach from that identification.

Another important aspect of not taking things personally is to practice forgiveness. When you're able to forgive others for their actions and opinions, you're freeing yourself from the burden of holding onto anger and resentment. This can be a powerful step in moving beyond the ego and embracing your True Self.

It's important to recognize that your sense of self is not fixed or static. Your identity is constantly evolving and changing based on your experiences and interactions with others. By recognizing this, you can begin to let go of your attachment to a fixed identity and embrace the fluidity of your True Self.

Ultimately, the idea of not taking things personally is about recognizing that we're all interconnected and that our actions and words have an impact on others. When we see ourselves as part of a greater whole, we're more likely to act with compassion and empathy toward others.

At the same time, it's important to recognize that not everyone will share your beliefs or values. You can't control how others perceive you or how they may react to you. What you can control is how you choose to respond to those interactions. By choosing to not take things personally, you can respond with love and understanding rather than defensiveness and anger.

The practice of not taking things personally can also help you cultivate a greater sense of inner peace and contentment. When you're not constantly seeking validation and approval from others, you're able to find a deeper sense of fulfillment from within. This can lead to a greater sense of happiness and well-being in your life.

The most important thing you can do is to remember that you're part of a greater whole. By recognizing your interconnectedness and embracing your True Self, you begin to let go of the need to take things personally and embrace a greater sense of peace and unity.

Take things personally, a misstep made,
Reality mistaken, a false view,
No person, just beliefs, a life portrayed,
Others' thoughts, so meaningless, won't ensue.

Opinions won't provoke nor judgments sway,
Unlikely claims which appear so sincere,
Each motion it makes holds you now at bay,
A false notion protected now so dear.

Free from constraints identity is split,
True Self, wholeness, totality now found,
Forgiveness comes as love's one true orbit,
Perfect extension, in love now abound.

Not just for you but for others as well,
No actual "you" or "other" to see,
Only love exists, as words do foretell,
God's truth and love live forever to be.

Projections of the Split-Mind

There's someone in my life right now who is reacting violently to the awakening I'm experiencing. What suggestions do you have to bring peace to this situation?

I now open to the Master Teacher within and the Whole Mind that is forever my own.

The more you activate and realize the inner Self that exists beyond all the changing forms of the world, the stronger other people will react to your presence. Those who are on the threshold of the awakening will be drawn to you, while anyone still hiding within the projection of their split-mind will react violently, rejecting you in order to maintain their own identity. Don't be surprised if this happens. Most of all, remember that their reaction is their own and has nothing to do with you. Bless them and send them on their way because they're not ready for the expansion required to dissolve the ego-mind.

It's important to remember that the reactions of others are not a reflection of your own worth or value. Their reactions are a projection of their own fears and insecurities as they struggle to hold onto their own identity in the face of our expanding consciousness.

You can respond to these reactions with compassion and understanding, recognizing that everyone is on their own unique path and at their own stage of awakening. Rather than taking their rejection personally, you can send them love and blessings, knowing that their journey will continue in its own time.

It's also important to recognize that your own awakening is a continual process, and you'll face your own challenges and obstacles along the way. As you encounter these challenges, you can use them as opportunities to deepen your understanding and connection with your True Self.

One of the keys to activating and realizing your inner Self is to cultivate a practice of mindfulness and presence. By staying present in each moment you can begin to connect with the deeper aspects of your being and tap into your inner wisdom and intuition.

You can also cultivate a sense of detachment from the changing forms of the world, recognizing that your True Self exists beyond the limitations of the physical world. By letting go of your attachment to external forms, you can connect with the deeper aspects of your being and tap into a greater sense of peace and freedom.

As you continue to awaken, you may notice that your relationships with others begin to shift and change. Some relationships may fall away, while new connections may arise. This is a natural part of the process as you begin to connect with others on a deeper level and align with those who are also on the path of awakening.

At times, you may feel isolated or alone on your journey. It's important to remember that you're never truly alone since you're always connected to the larger whole of existence. By staying connected to this deeper sense of connection, you can find the strength and support you need to continue on your path.

It's also important to recognize that the process of awakening is not always easy or comfortable. You may face challenges and obstacles that require you to step out of your comfort zone and confront your fears and limitations. By embracing these challenges, you can continue to expand your awareness and connect with your True Self on a deeper level.

Ultimately, the process of awakening is about letting go of the limitations of the ego-mind and connecting with the deeper aspects of your being. As you do so, you can begin to tap into a greater sense of peace, joy, and fulfillment, and align with your true purpose in life.

As you move forward on your path, embrace the reactions of others with compassion and understanding, recognizing that everyone is on their own unique journey. Learn to cultivate a practice of mindfulness and presence, and let go of your attachment to the changing forms of the world. Continue to deepen your connection with your True Self, aligning with your highest purpose and potential in life.

To realize the inner Self, the key,
Beyond all forms which the world projects out,
Drawing in others unable to see,
Some will be violent, of this, there's no doubt.

Those hiding in the split-mind projection,
Rejecting the light for fear of losing,
Maintain identity's false protection,
Then lashing out in violent refusing.

But know their reaction is but their own,
Not now a reflection of who you are,
Bless them and let them walk onward alone,
For none of them are ready to go far.

As we awaken others may react,
To our presence, strong emotions will rise,
Some so drawn others may choose to retract,
As we connect with our true self's own prize.

The Quickest Path to God

How would you describe the quickest path to God or whole-mindedness? You already shared that realizing the awakening is not only guaranteed but already complete as the ultimate goal. Can you speak more about that?

I now open to the Master Teacher within and the Whole Mind that is forever my own.

The quickest path to God is a persistent and passionate focus on the Presence of God as the Beloved. The Presence of God is all that exists, so focusing on anything other than this is an attempt to realize or experience all that isn't. This has been your goal from the beginning, the instant the idea of separation entered your mind. But it only entered the mind you think you think with.

The Presence of God as the Beloved is all that exists, and by focusing on it, you can realize the truth of your being and connect with the deeper aspects of your soul. When you focus on the Presence of God, you let go of all the distractions and illusions of the world. You recognize that the world is merely a projection of your own mind, and that True Reality lies beyond the physical forms you see around you.

By letting go of your attachment to the world, you create space for the Presence of God to enter your life. You begin to see the world in a new light, with fresh eyes and an open heart, and you discover a sense of peace and joy that you never knew was possible.

The Presence of God as the Beloved is the essence of your being, and by focusing on it you can awaken to your

True Nature and tap into a deeper sense of purpose and meaning in life.

This has been your goal from the beginning, the instant the idea of separation entered your mind. You've been searching for something or someone to fill the void that separation seems to have created, something to make you feel whole and complete once again. But the truth is that separation is an illusion, and the only way to truly find wholeness and completeness is to let go of the illusion and embrace the reality of your Oneness with All There Is, otherwise known as God.

When you focus on the Presence of God as the Beloved you begin to dissolve the illusion of separation and connect with the deeper aspects of your being. You discover that you're not separate from God, but rather a part of the larger whole of existence. This realization is the key to finding true fulfillment and purpose in life. It allows you to tap into a deeper sense of joy and contentment, and to live your life with greater clarity and intention.

It's important to remember that the mind you think with is not your Whole Mind. Your Whole Mind is the Mind of God, the infinite and eternal source of all that exists. By focusing on the Presence of God as the Beloved you align with this deeper aspect of your being and tap into a greater sense of wisdom and understanding. You begin to see the world in a new light, with fresh eyes and an open heart, and you discover a sense of peace and joy that you never knew was possible.

If you want to find God, focus persistently and passionately on the Presence of God as the Beloved. Let go of the illusions of the world and embrace the reality of your Oneness with the Divine. And know that as you do so, you're aligning with the deeper aspects of your being and tapping into a greater sense of purpose, meaning, and fulfillment in life.

The quickest path to God, a focus true,
Persistent, passionate, on God's Presence.
As the Beloved, all that is, all through,
Focusing on all else, a vain essence.

Your goal from the start was separation,
Thoughts that entered the mind with which you think.
To find God the truth of your foundation,
Focus on Presence and all else will shrink.

The Presence of God is all that exists,
Through passion and persistence, we connect,
While the deeper aspect of soul persists,
And truth of our being we resurrect.

Complete Certainty of Love's Power

Can you describe the most essential key for healing to take place?

I now open to the Master Teacher within and the Whole Mind that is forever my own.

Complete certainty of love's power is all that's needed to heal. Only one thing needs to be grasped - you're only healing illusions, so what difference does it make what illusion it is? It may appear as someone born blind. But human eyes were made not to see the Truth that is forever True. It may be someone suffering from a disease, but even this can be healed by the one who is certain of love's power.

Complete certainty of love's power is all that's needed to heal. When you understand that love is the most powerful force in the universe, you can begin to heal the illusions that have plagued you for so long.

The illusions that you face can take many different forms. It may be a physical illness that you're struggling with or a mental or emotional challenge that you're facing. Whatever the illusion may be, it's important to remember that it's not real.

In order to heal, you must recognize that these illusions are not part of your True Nature. They are simply distractions that have been placed in your path, designed to keep you from realizing your full potential.

But with love's power, you can overcome these illusions and find true healing. You can tap into the infinite energy of the universe and use it to transform your life in profound and meaningful ways.

The key to healing is to recognize that you're only healing illusions. You must let go of the attachments you have to the physical world and instead focus on the eternal truth that lies beyond the illusions.

Even if someone is born blind, this is simply an illusion that can be healed by seeing it as "already healed". The human eyes were made not to see the truth that is forever true, but with love's power, you can see beyond the illusions and tap into the deeper aspects of your being.

Similarly, even if someone is suffering from a disease, this too can be healed by the one who is completely certain of love's power. With the right mindset and a focus on the power of love, you can overcome any obstacle that stands in your way.

The most important thing to remember is that you're not alone in your healing journey. You're surrounded by the infinite love and energy of the universe, and when you tap into this energy, you can transform your life in amazing ways. It's also important to remember that the illusions you face are not random or meaningless. They are part of a larger plan that's designed to help you grow and evolve.

Through the process of healing, you can gain a deeper understanding of yourself and the world around you. You can tap into the infinite wisdom of the universe and discover your true purpose and calling in life.

If you want to experience true healing, focus on the power of love. Recognize that the illusions you face are not real and let go of the attachments that are holding you back. With a deep and abiding faith in the power of love, you can transform your life in amazing ways and experience true healing at every level of your being.

For love's power can transcend all pain and strife,
And bring us to a place of peace and Grace.
With certainty, we heal illusions rife,
And banish darkness with love's shining face.

The blind may now see with love's gentle touch,
And find a world of wonder and delight.
The sick may be healed by love's power so much,
And be restored to health and joy's bright light.

Complete certainty of love's power we need,
To heal the wounds that life so often brings.
With love as our guide, we now can proceed,
And rise above all earthly sufferings.

So let us grasp this truth and hold it tight,
That love is all we need to heal our pain.
With faith and hope, we'll banish every blight,
And find true happiness and peace again.

Rejection of Illusions

You speak of the I AM Presence as if it's always present and waiting for us to open to its power. Can you give me more detail on how I can listen to that voice to the exclusion of the ego?

I now open to the Master Teacher within and the Whole Mind that is forever my own.

The consciousness of I AM does not need to be affirmed by you to be wholly active in your life. It's wholly present and secure even in your sleeping state. What's required is a rejection of every illusion that's captured your mind. That's the key to listening only to the Voice of the I AM Presence within. You've used the power of the Name of God to identify with everything you are not. That's why the reduction of every limited form you've claimed as your identity is all that's required for the awakening.

For example, when you chant "I AM not a body," you're actually affirming the reality that is forever real within you. When you claim with certainty and power "I AM not a limited identity," you're actually affirming the fact that the truth within you can never be contained by a collection of concepts or ideas.

It's time to realize that your identity is really nothing more than a collection of concepts and ideas. Even if you collect or claim every concept in this world you still won't be close to the Truth that sleeps within you. Once again, the Truth within you doesn't need to be affirmed or even claimed. It already claimed you and that's the only thing you need to know.

The consciousness of I AM is always present within you, and it's this consciousness that connects you to the infinite nature of the universe. When you awaken to this truth you realize that you're not separate from anything. You're part of the infinite consciousness that flows through all of creation. This realization brings a deep sense of peace and understanding, and it allows you to let go of all the illusions that have been holding you back.

To awaken to the consciousness of I AM, you must first reject the illusions that have kept you in a state of separation. These illusions include your beliefs in your limited identity, your attachment to material possessions, and your identification with the world of form. Once you let go of these illusions, you'll be able to see the truth that has always been present within you.

The Truth of the consciousness of I AM is not something that needs to be affirmed or claimed, for it's already a part of your being. It's the power that creates and sustains all of creation, and it's always present within you, even when you're not aware of it. When you awaken to this truth you'll realize that you're not separate from anything and that you're part of the infinite consciousness that flows through all of creation.

To awaken to the consciousness of I AM you must be willing to let go of your attachment to the limited identity that you've created for yourself. This identity is based on the beliefs and opinions you've claimed for yourself, and it's the source of all your suffering. When you let go of this limited identity you'll be able to connect with the infinite consciousness that's always present within you.

The consciousness of I AM is not something that can be acquired or attained through effort. It's already present within you and it only needs to be recognized and acknowledged. When you awaken to this truth you'll realize that all of your efforts to achieve or acquire anything have been based on illusions, and that the truth of your being is already complete and perfect.

The consciousness of I AM is the source of all creation, and it's the power that sustains all life. When you awaken to this Truth, you'll realize that you're not separate from anything and that you're a part of the infinite consciousness that flows through all of creation. This realization brings a deep sense of peace and understanding, and it allows you to let go of all the illusions that have been holding you back.

The consciousness of I AM is the truth of your being, and it's the source of all creation. When you awaken to this truth you'll realize that you're not separate from anything and that you're part of the Infinite Consciousness that flows through all of creation. This realization brings a deep sense of peace and understanding, and it allows you to let go of all the illusions that have been holding you back.

The consciousness of I AM is not something that can be found outside of yourself. It's already present within you, and it only needs to be recognized and acknowledged. When you awaken to Reality this will not only be completely clear to your mind, but to your Whole Self.

The consciousness of I AM needs no proof,
Secure and present even as you sleep.
Illusions rejected, truth has no roof,
Awakening requires we dive so deep.

The power of God's name you have now misused,
Identifying with what you are not.
Limited forms claimed, your truth thus abused,
Reduction of falsehood is all you've got.

"I AM not a body," is now the way,
Affirm reality forever real.
"I AM not limited," you must now say,
To claim truth that no concept can seal.

No need to affirm, no need now to claim,
For truth within needs no affirmation.
The only thing to know already claimed,
The eternal I AM, your salvation.

A Workshop on Heaven

I recently saw a cartoon in a magazine that showed two doors - one door said "Heaven" and the other door said "Workshop on Heaven." A long line of people stood in front of the Workshop door but no one stood in front of the door that led directly into Heaven. Why is it so much easier to study the Truth rather than step into the Real World?

I now open to the Master Teacher within and the Whole Mind that is forever my own.

This is a very good question. You've spent so much time trying to find a workshop on Heaven instead of stepping through a door that's never been closed to you. Why not throw away every idea you've ever had and let Heaven rush through the open window of your heart? Throwing away every idea or concept of the ego is the only thing left for you to do. Once you do you'll realize that neither the door marked "Heaven" or "Workshop on Heaven" are real. That will be the same Holy Instant of your release into eternity.

You still think there's work to be done. There isn't. You still believe there's something you lack, the reception of which would give you the key to open the gate you believe is closed. All I'm telling you is that the gate was never closed. All I'm trying to get you to see is that there's no workshop on Heaven that will get you to where you already are. Did you hear that? You're already in Heaven so why would you need a workshop?

All you need is to open your eyes and see where you are. The only requirement is for you to open your mind and remember who you are. You are the holy perfect extension of the perfect love of God. Isn't that enough? Why would you search for more than ALL THERE IS? A Whole Mind is simply one that stops searching when the treasure has been found. A Master Teacher is someone who realizes the futility of trying to gain something that was never lost or accomplish something that was already accomplished.

Enlightenment is the simple, passionate recognition of the You that never gave any credit to the you you thought you created. That's the only thing you still haven't done - stop giving credit to the you you thought you created, but give total credit to the You that was created by God. This is why the awakening is so simple - you never actually fell asleep. You only closed your eyes for an instant and the instant that happened the terrible thought of separation was healed. The world you thought you saw was never the Real World where you're truly at home.

You spend so much time trying to find a way to reach Heaven, as if it were a distant place, when in fact, it is right here within you. You're already in the Kingdom of Heaven but you've closed your eyes to it. It's time to stop searching for a workshop or a guide to lead you there because the door has never been closed. It's only your perception that's been closed.

Throw away all the ideas and concepts you've ever had about Heaven, and let the truth reveal itself to you. There's nothing you need to do or work for because everything you seek is already present within you. All you need do is open your heart and let the light of Heaven shine in.

You may believe that there's something you lack or something you need to acquire to gain entrance into Heaven, but this is an illusion. In fact, it's the greatest illusion. The truth is so simple: you're already whole and complete, lacking nothing. It's only your false beliefs that make you think otherwise.

The key to accessing Heaven is not found in any workshop or book. It's found within your own being. You're a holy and perfect extension of the love of God, and this is all you need to remember. You don't need to search for anything outside of yourself because you already have everything you need within.

All that's required of you is to open your mind and remember who you truly are. You're not a limited human being, but a Divine being who is capable of experiencing the limitless love and joy of the Kingdom of Heaven. Once you remember this truth you'll see that the gate to Heaven has always been open.

Enlightenment is not something that you need to strive for, but something that you already possess. It's the recognition of the Truth of who you are and the letting go of all the false beliefs that have been holding you back. When you realize that you're already in Heaven, everything else falls away.

Stop searching for something that you already have. Stop trying to accomplish something that's already been accomplished. Instead, simply rest in the knowledge that you're a perfect and holy extension of the love of God. This is all you need to be happy and fulfilled.

The awakening is simple because you never really fell asleep. You only closed your eyes to the truth of who you are for the briefest second. But that second has passed and now it's time to open your eyes and see the Truth. You're already in Heaven and nothing can ever change that.

The world you thought you saw was never the Real World. It was only a projection of your own mind. But now that you've opened your eyes you can see the Truth of who you are and the reality of the Kingdom of Heaven that's already within you.

Just let go of all your doubts and fears and step through the door that has always been open. Let Heaven rush through the open window of your heart and embrace the Truth of who you are. You're already in Heaven and nothing can ever change that.

Why search for a workshop the door's ajar?
Let Heaven rush through your heart's open gate.
Discard every thought both near and so far,
Embrace your True Self, your Heavenly state.

You think there's work to be done yet there's none,
No key required to open unlocked doors.
The gate was never closed, the battle won,
Already in Heaven, forevermore.

Why seek a workshop when you're in the place?
Open your eyes and see what's always been.
No need for more work, no searching's the case,
Simply remember and let the truth in.

Open your mind and let the light shine through,
Remember who you are your true essence.
In Heaven's embrace, you'll find love that's true,
A perfect state now of purest presence.

An Irresistible Truth

I know that the Truth is simple and is easily attained once I release all the strange ideas that seem to have limited me. Is there anything you can share that's so normal and mundane that makes this even more clear?

I now open to the Master Teacher within and the Whole Mind that is forever my own.

If you could, how would you describe a sneeze? You might say that it's irresistible, or when it's finally achieved it's beyond satisfying. Or perhaps you'll remember a time when you were close to sneezing, but it never came. What did you feel? Did you feel as if you were robbed or deprived of something you wanted with your whole being?

It's obviously a ridiculous comparison, but this is what the experience of enlightenment is like. Remembering who you are is irresistible and there's nothing in this world that can compare to it. But even the hint of this memory without the final experience is beyond frustrating. You've come so close yet your mind still tells you that you're not "Everything." You believe that you're "nothing," or at best you're "something." But the "something" you believe yourself to be could never come close to the wholeness that you are in Truth. The limited idea you have of yourself is not even close to the unlimited reality God has of you. So who will you trust, your own weak attempts at proving your limited existence, or God's proclamation of your unlimited holiness? As always, the choice is yours.

Enlightenment is a state of being that's beyond the grasp of the human mind. It's like trying to describe the color blue to someone who's never seen it before. It's a state of pure joy, peace, and love that transcends all limitations of the human experience. It's a state of complete Oneness with everything and everyone around you, and there's nothing in this world that can compare.

The experience of enlightenment is like a sneeze that you can't help but let out. It's irresistible and beyond satisfying. It's the realization that you're one with the Divine and that everything in this world is an expression of that Divinity. It's the recognition that you're not separate from anything or anyone, but rather, you're part of the fabric of the universe.

The journey to enlightenment requires a willingness to face your fears and let go of all that's not aligned with the truth of who you are. It requires a willingness to confront the illusions that you've created in your mind and to see them for what they are. It requires a willingness to surrender your will to a higher power and to trust in the process of awakening.

The experience of enlightenment is not something that can be achieved through intellectual understanding or knowledge. I know I've said this many times already but its importance cannot be overlooked. Enlightenment a state of being that's beyond the limitations of the human mind. It's a state of pure awareness and presence that can only be experienced through direct realization.

The journey to enlightenment is a journey of self-discovery and self-realization. It's a journey of uncovering the Truth of who you are and letting go of all that is not in alignment with that Truth. It's a journey of surrender and trust, of letting go of the need to control and allowing yourself to be guided by a higher power.

The experience of enlightenment is a state of being that's available to all of us. It's not reserved for a select few, but rather, it's the birthright of every human being. It's the recognition that we're all one, and that there's no separation between us.

The journey to enlightenment is not a destination, but rather, it's a continual process of awakening. It's a process of shedding the layers of conditioning and programming that have kept you in a state of illusion and separation. It's a process of uncovering the truth of who you are and living from that truth.

The experience of enlightenment is the recognition that we're all one. It's the recognition that we're all connected and that there's no separation between us. It's the recognition that we're all expressions of the Divine and that we're here to serve a higher purpose.

The journey to enlightenment is a journey of love. It's a journey of learning to love ourselves and others unconditionally. It's a journey of learning to see the Divine in everyone and everything around us. It's a journey of learning to live from a place of love and compassion.

The experience of enlightenment is like a sneeze that you can't help but let out. It's the recognition that you're one with the Divine and there's no separation between you and everything that truly exists.

How to describe a sneeze, a simple act?
Irresistible satisfied release.
A moment of relief, a perfect fact.
Or frustration when the sneeze then does cease.

When compared to enlightenment, absurd,
The thought of who you truly are, Divine.
Irresistible, a calling that's heard,
Beyond true experience, undefined.

The hint of this thought is so very close,
The mind is still holding onto belief.
Not "Everything," as the truth it does oppose,
A self-image, God's view, beyond belief.

Trust in the weak attempts of your own thought?
Or God's proclamation holiness true?
Limited life these illusions you've wrought,
Unlimited life of God to pursue.

The choice is yours, the decision to make,
To remember who you are in this light.
In God's full embrace your soul will awake,
A journey of love and truth taking flight.

The Power of Devotion

So many people try to understand these Truths through the mind, and there has to be some value in that, even though it's limited. In the yogic tradition, the intellectual aspect of awakening is honored, but nowhere near the value given to Bhakti Yoga, or the yoga of devotion. Can you speak more about these differences?

I now open to the Master Teacher within and the Whole Mind that is forever my own.

A scholar is taken aback by the ecstatic experience of a saint, thinking that intellectual knowledge is the key to spiritual understanding. But a saint knows that true understanding comes from direct experience of the Divine. The Name of God, I AM, is not just a mental exercise or a mantra to recite, but a living expression of the Divine that has the power to transform your consciousness. A scholar may understand the theory of the Name, but the saint has the direct experience of its power through love and devotion.

The same is true for all spiritual practices. They're not meant to be just intellectual exercises or rituals to follow, but a means to connect with the Divine in a direct and personal way. The power of the Name of God lies not in the repetition of words, but in the intention behind them. A sincere longing for God activates the power of the Name and opens the door to the Divine.

The journey to the Divine is not an intellectual pursuit, but a journey of the heart. It's a journey of longing, of yearning for the Beloved. The heart is the gateway to the Divine, and it's through the heart that you can experience the Divine directly. The heart is the seat of your deepest desires, and when you turn your desires toward the Divine, you begin to experience the fullness of the Divine in your life.

The repetition of the Name of God is not a technique, but a surrender to God. It's a way of letting go of the limited self and allowing the Divine to enter and transform you. It's a way of saying to God, "I AM yours, do with me what you will." In this surrender, you open yourself to infinite possibilities.

The repetition of the Name of God is not just a means to an end, but a way of life. It's a way of living in constant remembrance of the Divine. It's a way of bringing the Presence of God into every moment of your life. It's a way of living in a state of Grace where every action is infused with the Divine Light.

The Name of God is not just words, but a living expression of Divinity. It's a way of opening the heart and allowing the Divine to enter. It's a way of experiencing the fullness of the Divine in your life. It's a way of living in constant remembrance of God. It's a way of surrendering to the Beloved and allowing the Divine to transform you.

The repetition of any Name of God is not a practice that can be taught or learned, but a way of being that must be experienced. It's a way of living in the Divine Presence and allowing the Beloved to guide you. It's a way of living in a state of Grace and experiencing the fullness of the Divine in your life.

The journey to the Divine is not a journey at all, but a remembering of who you truly are. It's a remembering of your Divine Nature which is always present and always available. It's a surrender to the Beloved and a letting go of the limited self. It's a way of living in a state of Grace where every moment is infused with the Divine.

The path to the Divine starts in the heart,
Not in the mind with logic as its chart.
A journey of longing, yearning for love,
Gateway to the Divine sent from above.

The heart holds desires deepest and pure,
When turning toward God, the soul can endure.
For in the heart, we do know the Divine,
Through love, compassion, and pure Grace so fine.

Repeating God's Name, not a mere technique,
But a surrender, a way now to seek
The Divine's will, to let go and to be,
A vessel for love, a soul truly free.

The Name is not just a means to an end,
But a way of life, a path to transcend.
The mundane, the ego, and all that's low,
Into a state of Grace where love will flow.

ALL Are Holy Because One is Only

Speak to me about the holiness that rests within each of us. It seems that this is the core message. But it's also clear that I'm the only one who has to embrace this Reality, not wait for others to do it. These two ideas seem to contradict each other but I can see now that they're the same.

I now open to the Master Teacher within and the Whole Mind that is forever my own.

One is holy only if all are holy; and because ALL are holy, One is only. Herein lies the undoing of all error.

This statement is of fundamental importance. It suggests that holiness is not an individual characteristic but rather an inherent quality of all creation. It further implies that the individual experience of holiness is not possible unless everyone experiences it.

The idea that all are holy can be challenging to grasp, especially when you look around yourself and see people behaving in ways that are not aligned with your understanding of holiness. However, holiness is not something that you achieve or earn through good deeds or spiritual practice, but something that's given to you by God.

In other words, your holiness is not dependent on your behavior, but is an inherent quality of your being, given to you by your Creator. The only thing that stands in the way of perfect awareness of your eternal holiness is your identification with the ego, which is the false self you've created to protect yourself from the fear and pain of separation from God.

The ego is the source of all error, which is any thought or belief that's not aligned with your True Nature. This includes beliefs in separation, sin, guilt, and fear. The only way to undo these errors is through forgiveness, which is the process of letting go of your identification with the ego and remembering your True Identity as the holy perfect creation of a wholly perfect Creator.

When you recognize that all are holy, you're acknowledging that your true nature is not separate from the true nature of anyone else. This recognition is the foundation of true forgiveness, which is the process of releasing your judgments and grievances against yourself and others.

When you forgive, you're recognizing that the errors you see in others are simply a reflection of the errors you hide within yourself, and that by releasing your judgments, you're releasing yourself from the bondage of the ego.

The statement "One is holy only if all are holy; and because ALL are holy, One is only. Herein lies the undoing of all error" teaches that holiness is not an individual characteristic, but an inherent quality of all creation. It further suggests that the only way to experience your own holiness is to recognize holiness in everyone else. By doing so, you can release yourself from the bondage of the ego and experience the oneness that is your True nature.

In Oneness there is no separation,
For all is holy, every soul and being.
The ego's hold, the source of delusion,
Is shattered by this truth, all error freeing.

The One, the holy, only can exist,
When all are holy, every single soul.
The unity of being can't be missed,
For every part makes the whole, the true goal.

This truth undoes the mind's illusions vast,
That would convince us of separation.
For in the One, we find our peace at last,
And every error meets its end, cessation.

So let us embrace this truth in our hearts,
And know that we are holy, every one.
For in this Oneness no illusion starts,
For we are the free, holy, perfect Son.

The Holy Instant We Share

On the subject of longing, it's clear that both the soul and the ego long for their unique and particular goal - The goal of the soul being to experience uncompromised Oneness, and the ego being to block the experience of that same Oneness. Can you speak more about how these two differ and how the goal of the soul can be achieved?

I now open to the Master Teacher within and the Whole Mind that is forever my own.

Your Soul, beyond all time and space, longs for nothing since it looks upon everything that's real and claims it as its own. It's secure within this reality and radiates the same, just as the sun is secure within itself and radiates its light, giving birth to planets and all life. And so are you giving birth to the Holy Instant we share, and because we share it, it increases for all. What seemed to retract now expands, and since this sacred expansion has no end, it extends forever and forever.

Your identity, or who you believe yourself to be, constantly longs for more of what it does not have because it's insecure within its own unreality. It gathers and it claims, but nothing assures it of its safety. That's because it's never safe within the world it created to hide from reality. It finds security in being hidden, but now the Light has come and you can hide no more. Step out of the shadows, Holy Perfect Child of God, and see the Heaven that was reserved for you before time ever began.

Your soul is connected to everything that is real. It's not bound by the limitations of your physical body or your current life circumstances. It's an eternal, timeless essence that transcends all human understanding. Your soul is the source of your inner wisdom and intuition, and it holds the key to your deepest desires and dreams.

When you connect with your soul, you tap into a wellspring of creativity and inspiration that can help you manifest your true potential. Your soul is the guiding force that leads you toward your highest purpose in life, and it provides you with the courage and strength to overcome any obstacle that may come your way.

As you align with your soul's purpose, you begin to experience a sense of peace and fulfillment that goes beyond anything you've ever known. You realize that you're part of something greater than yourself, and that your existence has a profound meaning and purpose. You feel a deep sense of connection with all of life, and you begin to see the world through the eyes of love and compassion.

Your soul is the light that guides you through the darkness of this world. It's the spark that ignites your passion for life and gives you the courage to follow your dreams. Your soul is the wellspring of your inner strength and resilience, and it enables you to overcome the challenges that come your way.

When you're in touch with your soul you live a life of purpose and meaning. You're driven by a deep sense of love and compassion for all living beings, and you seek to make a positive difference in the world. Your soul is the source of your inspiration and creativity, and it enables you to express yourself in unique and meaningful ways.

Your soul is the essence of who you are, and it holds the key to your highest potential. When you're in alignment with your soul you're able to tap into a wellspring of wisdom and insight that can help you to overcome any obstacle that comes your way. Your soul is the guiding force that leads you toward your highest purpose in life, and it provides you with the courage and strength to achieve your dreams.

Your soul is the source of true power and it enables you to live a life of abundance and prosperity. When you're in touch with your soul you're able to attract positive experiences and opportunities into your life, and you're able to manifest your deepest desires and dreams. Your soul is the driving force behind your success, and it empowers you to live a life of purpose and meaning.

Your soul is the foundation of your being, and it holds the key to your inner peace and happiness. When you're in touch with your soul you're able to experience a sense of peace and tranquility that goes beyond anything you've ever known. You're able to let go of stress and worry, and you're able to live in the present moment with a sense of ease and Grace.

Your soul is the light that illuminates your path in life, and it enables you to navigate even the most challenging circumstances with ease and Grace. When you're in touch with your soul you're able to experience a deep sense of trust and faith in the universe, and you know that everything is working out for your highest good. Your soul is the guiding force that leads you toward your highest potential, and it empowers you to live a life of purpose and meaning.

Your Soul, beyond all time and space, does shine,
Looking upon all that is real, Divine.
It claims its own, secure within this place,
Radiating the same like sun's bright shine.

The sun gives birth to the Instant we share,
Expanding beyond time reflections glare.
Undoing all error it expands without fear,
Growing larger expanding with love's care.

This identity who you think to be,
Constantly seeks more but never is free.
Insecurity creeps, you are not free,
But the Light has come, reveals clarity.

Step out of the shadows, God's Child Divine,
See Heaven that's yours, before time's design.
Claiming your place now in Love's holy shrine,
You are so holy, forever Divine.

Identity Begins to Fade

Protecting the body and identity seems to be the highest goal of the ego. As long as we're in physical form it's hard to bypass this focus. Are there any steps we can take that will help speed up our eventual release from the split-mind?

I now open to the Master Teacher within and the Whole Mind that is forever my own.

The activity of all living beings is to sustain Beingness. Until realization of Self occurs this is interpreted as sustaining or protecting the body and identity. Once liberation from the split-self has been achieved, protecting the body and identity becomes a non-issue. The body will do what the body will do and the identity that seems to be separate from all other identities will begin to dissolve. This is what's known as freedom from self. Once again, until you fully release your body-identity this will seem like death, and so it shall be. But the instant you seek only the gifts of Heaven and deny the constraints of this world, you'll realize the Truth that has always been True, and the Reality that has always been Real.

Isn't this what you really want? Unfortunately the answer is no. You've wanted so many things and set your desire upon chains that bind rather than wings that fly. Why would you do this unless you're afraid of flying? Begin by admitting that you're content with chains because you still believe that you're guilty of a sin that never occurred in reality. Does it help to know that such a thing is impossible?

Guilt belongs to the guilty, and yet you are wholly innocent of sin. But you won't realize this until you offer the gift of guiltlessness to everyone you see or think of. Hold it back from anyone and you deny your Self. Why would you continue doing this when it's never given you what you really want? Only love can do this, and love will only come if you forgive everyone and everything, including and most especially yourself.

You must release your past and your judgments of it if you want to experience the freedom that comes with forgiveness. The past is over and gone, and yet you continue to drag it around with you as if it has some significance in the present. It only has significance if you give it significance. Let it go and you'll see that the present moment is all that's real.

When you release the past and forgive everyone you'll experience a shift in your perception. You'll see the world as it truly is, a reflection of the love that you are. You'll see that everyone and everything is a part of you and that you are a part of everything. This is the realization of Oneness, the experience of the non-dual reality.

As you continue to forgive and release, you'll experience a deepening sense of peace and joy. You'll no longer be burdened by the weight of the past, and you'll be able to fully embrace the present moment. Your soul will be free to express itself in whatever way it chooses, and you'll experience a sense of creative freedom that you may never have known before.

This creative freedom is not limited to any particular form of expression. You may find that you're drawn to music, art, writing, or any other form of creative expression. Whatever form it takes, it will be a reflection of the love that you are and an expression of your soul.

In this state of freedom and creative expression, you'll find that you're able to manifest your desires with ease. You'll no longer be held back by limiting beliefs and judgments, and you'll be able to tap into the infinite abundance of the universe.

As you continue to release and forgive you'll find that your experience of life becomes richer and more fulfilling. You'll be able to connect with others on a deeper level, and you'll be able to see the beauty in everything and everyone.

The goal of this journey is to realize the truth of who you are. You are not the body or the identity that you've believed yourself to be. You're the love that underlies all of existence, the essence of all that is. When you realize this truth, you'll experience a sense of Oneness with everything and everyone, and you'll know that there is nothing to fear or to protect.

In this state of realization, you'll be able to fully embrace the present moment and experience the fullness of life. You'll no longer be limited by the past or the future, and you'll be able to fully express the love that you are in everything you do.

Release the chains that bind you and embrace the wings that will take you to the heights of your soul's expression. The journey may seem daunting, but the rewards are beyond measure. Trust in the love that you are, and let it guide you to the truth that has always been within you.

The quest for Beingness guides each one all,
Until the Self we know and can recall.
We strive to keep the body safe and sound,
And guard the ego's separate self we found.

But once we're freed from this illusion's hold,
The body's fate we'll no longer behold.
Our ego's chains will start to slip away,
As we embrace the Truth and choose to stay.

This freedom from the self may seem like death,
But it's the chance to draw a brand-new breath.
For in this moment, we can truly see,
The gifts of Heaven and our destiny.

Yet still, we hesitate and cling to chains,
Content to live within our self-made pains.
We fear to fly and soar above it all,
Held back by guilt and shame's relentless call.

But know, dear soul, that sin cannot exist,
And it's this Truth that we must now insist.
The chains that bind us we can cast aside,
And spread our wings to soar, to live, to glide.

Let the World Be the World

It's easy to admit that God is the creative force that unites the universe, at least intellectually. But grasping this intellectually isn't the goal. The goal is to have a full experience of this reality. Opening our spiritual eyes is clearly the first step. Is there anything else you'd like to add to that?

I now open to the Master Teacher within and the Whole Mind that is forever my own.

As you begin to see the creative force behind everything, you'll also begin to see the interconnectedness of all things. You'll see that everything is in a state of constant flux, always changing and evolving in dynamic ways. Nothing is ever truly static or separate from anything else.

In this state of perception, you'll be able to let go of the need to control or manipulate the world around you. You'll see that the world is perfectly capable of taking care of itself and that you're a part of its natural flow. You'll be able to let go of the struggle and resistance that comes with trying to control your surroundings.

When you let go of the need to control you'll also let go of fear. Fear arises from the belief that you're separate from the world and that you must protect yourself from it. When you see that you're a part of the whole and that the creative force behind everything is within you, fear will dissipate and finally vanish.

This doesn't mean that you'll never experience fear or discomfort again, but rather that you'll be able to see it for what it is and move through it with greater ease. You'll be able to see the bigger picture and the lessons that are being offered to you, rather than getting lost in fear and confusion.

In this state of perception, you'll also be able to see the beauty and wonder of the world around you. You'll see that everything is infused with creative force and that even the smallest things are miracles in their own right. You'll be able to appreciate the richness and diversity of life and see the interconnectedness of everything.

Let your hold on the world be tenuous and allow yourself to see everything with soft eyes. Open yourself to the creative force behind everything and trust in its natural flow. Let go of the need to control or manipulate, and embrace the beauty and wonder of life. In doing so, you'll experience a profound sense of peace and connectedness, and will be able to live in harmony with the world around you.

Let your grip on the world be light and free,
With gentle eyes observe all that you see.
And in this way you'll come to comprehend,
The force behind creation without end.

The world you see is not all that exists,
There's something more beyond what it enlists.
It's the creative power that lies within,
The spark that ignites all things to begin.

Look closer with a tender softened gaze,
You'll find beauty in unexpected ways.
Each creation holds sacred energy,
A glimpse of the Divine's great synergy.

So loosen your grip, let your heart be light,
Embrace the wonder of each day and night.
For in this way, you'll come to understand,
The force of creation at your command.

There is No Problem to Solve

You've said before that the ego perceives problems in the world and then tries to solve them where they can't be found - outside rather than within; while a Whole Mind looks past the outer circumstance and completely disregards the outer evidence. Speak to me further on how we can make that choice and shift into the soul's perspective of Oneness.

I now open to the Master Teacher within and the Whole Mind that is forever my own.

A healed or Whole Mind never looks for the solution to a problem within the world of form. In fact, a healed or Whole Mind never even looks for the problem within the world. It's like searching for a rare gem in your dream but then you wake up the instant you discover it. Are you any richer for having found a priceless jewel while asleep and dreaming?

There's nothing in this world that can contain you, just as there's nothing in this world that will never satisfy you. Seek what you will, but don't expect a true change to occur. You may set your mind on attracting the perfect mate, and you may even accomplish the task. You may work for years to save enough money to buy the house of your dreams, but don't expect the house to ever leave your dream. Whatever is born within a dream stays within the dream, but that which lies beyond your imagined world remains unchanged forever. Most of all, you remain unchanged forever, perfect in your holiness. Seek only this realization and experience, then the dream figures that once attracted you will fade and dissolve, and all you'll be left with is your Self.

The world is like a mirage that disappears when you approach it. You may believe that the solution to your problems lies in the world, but the world is only a reflection of your mind. When you heal your mind, the world becomes a reflection of your wholeness. The problems that once seemed insurmountable will disappear like the mirage, and all that remains is the peace of God.

A healed mind healed perceives the world in a different way. It no longer sees the world as a place of scarcity and lack but as a place of abundance and love. It no longer seeks to take from the world but to give to it. It no longer seeks to be special or unique but to recognize its Oneness with all that is.

When you look upon the world with a healed mind you see the creative force behind everything. You see the beauty in everything, even in the things that were once ugly or unappealing. You see the wholeness in everything, even in the things that were once broken or incomplete. You see the love in everything, even in the things that were once hateful or fearful.

The healed mind knows that it's not separate from the world, but is one with it. It knows that it's not a victim of the world, but the creator of it. It knows that it's not bound by the limitations of the world, but is free to transcend them. It knows that it's not a body that's separate from the world, but a spirit that's one with it.

When your mind is healed you'll no longer look for the solution to your problems in the world of form. You know that the solution lies within your mind and you're willing to accept the truth that's already there. You no longer try to fix the world, but you allow the world to be a reflection of your wholeness. You no longer try to change the world, but you allow the world to change through your loving presence.

The only thing that truly matters is the realization of your wholeness. All the things that you once thought were important will fade away, and all that will be left is your love for God and your love for all that is. The world will no longer hold any appeal for you because you'll know that it's only a reflection of your mind. You'll be content to rest in the peace of God, knowing that you're One with all that is.

A mind made Whole seeks not in forms or things,
For Truth it finds beyond what matter brings.
No search for problems in this realm of form,
For such illusions cannot cause true harm.

A rare gem in a dream may seem so grand,
But once awake, it slips away like sand.
Thus, a healed Mind knows the search is in vain,
For all in form is but a fleeting strain.

No riches found in dreams can truly last,
Nor solve the problems that we hold so fast.
The true solution lies beyond the veil,
Where Love and Truth and Beauty never fail.

So let your Whole Mind soar beyond the dream,
Where illusions fade - Truth begins to gleam.
No longer bound by form, it finds its rest,
In Love Divine the source of all that's best.

An Unchangeable Truth

There doesn't seem to be anything consistent in the physical world, but you've said that the Real World is perfectly consistent. Can you speak more about that?

I now open to the Master Teacher within and the Whole Mind that is forever my own.

You look at the world and what do you see? Is there anything consistent here? Can you find anything that remains the same forever? The world you perceive is the opposite of eternal and changeless, and the mind you use to see this unstable world sees changelessness as undesirable, even boring. Can you relate to this at all?

All I can tell you is that the Truth within you can never change, never ends, and the experience of this Truth is anything but boring. It's up to you to look upon this or choose the illusions that seem to oppose Reality. You may choose to look upon the body that grows old and say: "this is real…this is who I am," but that doesn't make it so. You may choose to look upon the world and say: "this is the way of things…to die and decay," but that doesn't make it so. There's an experience of Self that exists beyond the reach of all this. You are that Self, and that Self alone knows love. This Self alone is perfectly consistent in all its thoughts, knows Its Creator, understands Itself, is perfect in Its knowledge and Its love, and never changes from Its constant state of union with Its Creator and Itself. This is who you are in Reality, and it's who you will always be.

So the choice you believe you have is really no choice at all. You'll inevitably choose love because it's what you are in Truth, and you cannot claim what you are in illusions forever. Why not NOW!

It's true that choosing love and the Truth may seem difficult at times, but this difficulty is only because of the illusions you've held onto for so long. The ego has convinced you that the world of form is all there is, and it takes great effort to release this belief. But once you've made the choice to see beyond illusions, everything else will fall away effortlessly.

The moment you realize that the world of form is not real and does not define you, you'll experience a profound sense of peace and freedom. You'll recognize that you're not limited by the body, the mind, or the circumstances of your life. You'll see that you're a limitless being, connected with all of creation and that you have access to infinite wisdom and power.

It's important to remember that the world of form can never satisfy your deepest longings. No matter how much money, success, or fame you attain, there will always be a sense of emptiness within you. This emptiness can only be filled by the Truth, by connecting to your True Self and to the Creator of all that exists.

As you continue on your journey toward Truth you'll begin to recognize the signs and messages that are guiding you along the way. You'll see that everything that's happening in your life is serving a purpose and that each experience is an opportunity for growth and learning. You'll learn to trust the process and surrender to the wisdom of the Universe.

The more you align with the Truth the more you'll be able to discern the illusions of the world. You'll recognize the ego's tricks and be able to release them easily. You'll be able to see beyond the surface level of things and understand the deeper meaning of life.

Remember that you're not alone on this journey. There is a higher power that's guiding you, supporting you, and loving you every step of the way. You're never separate from this power and you can tap into it at any time. Trust that you're always where you need to be and that everything is happening for your highest good.

The world you see is only a reflection of your own thoughts and beliefs. If you want to change the world you must first change your mind. You must let go of the illusions that are keeping you stuck and embrace the Truth that is always available to you.

The choice to see beyond illusions is the most important choice you'll ever make. It's the choice to awaken to your True Self and to the love that's your birthright. This choice is always available to you and you can make it at any moment. All it takes is a willingness to let go of illusions and embrace the Truth.

Remember that the Truth is not something that can be found outside of you. It's already within you, waiting to be uncovered. All you need to do is let go of the illusions that are covering it up. When you do, you'll experience a profound sense of peace, joy, and love that will never fade.

Take the first step on this journey today. Choose to see beyond the illusions and embrace the Truth. Trust that you're always supported and guided and that you're never alone. Remember that you're a limitless being, connected to all of creation, and that you have access to infinite wisdom and power. The Truth is waiting for you, and it will always be there, whenever you're ready to receive it.

You gaze upon the world, what do you see?
Is anything the same consistently?
The world you know is inconstant and frail,
Your mind sees changelessness as dull and stale.

Truth within you can never change or die,
Experience of it you can't deny,
It's up to you to choose the Truth or see,
This Truth will set you free, eternally.

You may think the body is who you are,
Or see death and decay and call it law,
But beyond it all, there's a Self that knows,
Love, constant in thoughts, perfect in Its flows.

This Self united with the Creator,
And with Itself, perfect love forever,
It knows its purpose and understands all,
This is who you are beyond the world's thrall.

Impossible to Lose

The thought of loss keeps coming into my mind. What will I lose if I give everything to this teaching? I know you've said that it's impossible to lose what is true. Can you go into this a bit deeper so I feel more relaxed in this awakening?

I now open to the Master Teacher within and the Whole Mind that is forever my own.

You cannot lose what was never yours. This thought alone is enough to break the chains that seem to bar you from Heaven. It's the same as saying that you can't give what never actually belonged to you. And yet, you can seem to do these things, and you'll even gather evidence to prove that you were successful. But that does not make it so, regardless of the so-called proof you seem to possess. You'll claim death as the proof that life is not eternal. Do you see how insane this is?

In Truth, there is no death, only the illusion of death. The body is not life. It's merely a vessel for life to express itself through. When the body dies life does not cease to exist, it merely transforms into a different form of expression. Life is eternal, and you are that life. You are not the body, nor are you the mind that identifies with the body. You are the life that animates the body and the mind, and that life is eternal.

When you recognize the eternal nature of your being, the fear of death loses its grip on you. You realize that there's nothing to fear because you can't lose what was never yours to begin with. You're not the body, and therefore, the death of the body is not the end of you.

You're the eternal life that animates the body, and that life cannot be destroyed.

Once you realize this Truth you'll be free of the fear of death and the illusions of the world. You'll recognize that everything in the world is temporary and fleeting, and that true fulfillment and lasting happiness can only be found in the eternal. You'll no longer seek for happiness and fulfillment in the world, but instead, you'll turn your attention inward to the eternal wellspring of joy and peace within you.

This shift in perception changes everything. You'll no longer identify with the body and the egoic mind that seeks for temporary pleasures and possessions. Instead, you'll identify with the eternal nature of your being, and you'll seek for the things that are eternal and unchanging. You'll seek for the experience of love, peace, and joy that comes from the realization of your True Nature.

As you continue to abide in the Truth of your being the illusions of the world lose their hold on you. You recognize that the things you once thought were important are actually meaningless, and the things you once thought were meaningless are actually important. You begin to see the world in a different light, and you realize that the purpose of your life is not to accumulate possessions or achieve status, but to awaken to the Truth of your being and to express that Truth in the world.

In this way, the recognition of the eternal nature of your being brings about a radical shift in your perception of the world and your place in it. You no longer see yourself as a separate entity struggling to survive in a hostile world, but as the eternal life that animates all things. You recognize that the world is not something to be conquered or controlled, but something to be celebrated and enjoyed.

As you continue to abide in the Truth of your being, you begin to see the world in a new light. You see the beauty and wonder that surrounds you, and you recognize that everything in the world is a reflection of the eternal beauty and wonder of your being. You see that the world is not something to be feared, but something to be loved and cherished.

In this way, the recognition of the eternal nature of your being brings about a profound shift in your relationship with the world. You no longer see the world as a hostile and dangerous place, but as a beautiful and wondrous expression of the eternal. You no longer seek to conquer or control the world, but to love and honor it. There's even a step beyond that, but that's for a later time.

As you continue to abide in the Truth of your being you realize that the illusions of the world are nothing more than a dream. You recognize that the world is not real in the way that you once thought it was, but a projection of your own mind. You see that the only thing that's real is the eternal nature of your being, and that everything else is just a passing dream.

In this way, the recognition of the eternal nature of your being brings about a profound shift in your relationship with the world. You no longer take the illusions as real but allow Reality to take its place, guiding you into the Heaven you never really left.

You think you possess what you cannot hold,
And cling to things that are not truly sold.
But these illusions can be shattered fast,
With just the thought that nothing here can last.

For what was never yours you cannot lose,
No matter how you try to chase or choose.
You gather proof to show now your success,
But in the end, it's all an empty dress.

Death seems to prove that life cannot endure,
But it's illusion that's hard to ensure.
The body, just a vessel for the soul,
Which never dies but finds a higher goal.

Life is eternal and you are its force,
Not just a body that will run its course.
So let go of the chains that bind you tight,
Embrace the Truth that sets your soul alight.

All Good is Forever Good

Everything you're sharing relates to an eternal, total experience that's completely beyond the world we seem to inhabit. And yet we still find ourselves in that world of limitation. Speak to me about the step beyond this world into the infinite.

I now open to the Master Teacher within and the Whole Mind that is forever my own.

You are the ALL good. ALL good! The ego is willing to consider the possibility of a partial good, seeing some people as good and others as not-good, but a total and complete good it will not endure. That's because the experience of a total and complete good would mean it's complete demise, or the dissolving of what it believes itself to be into All That IS.

The ego is not interested in experiencing true spiritual growth because that would mean surrendering control and allowing the Holy Spirit to guide you. The ego thrives on control and manipulation, and therefore it will do whatever it takes to maintain its perceived power. This is why true spiritual growth often requires great inner work and a willingness to let go of the old patterns and beliefs that no longer serve you.

However, once you begin to awaken to your True Nature as infinite spiritual consciousness, you realize that there's nothing to fear in letting go of the ego. In fact, the more you surrender to your Higher Self, the more peace and joy you experience in your life. You begin to see the world in a new light and are able to transcend the limitations of the ego.

It's important to note that spiritual growth is not about achieving a certain state of being or becoming "enlightened." It's about realizing that you're already perfect and whole, and that everything you need is already within you. It's about discovering your True Nature and living in alignment with that, rather than trying to mold yourself into something you are not.

This realization can be a bit daunting at first as it requires that you let go of the old stories and beliefs you've been telling yourself for so long. But the more you practice surrendering to your Higher Self the easier it becomes to live from a place of love and compassion rather than fear and control.

As you continue to awaken to your True Nature you begin to experience a sense of interconnectedness with all of life. You realize that you're not separate from anyone or anything, but rather we're all part of the same Divine consciousness. This realization leads to a deep sense of compassion and a desire to serve others and the world.

In order to fully embrace your True Nature as infinite spiritual consciousness you must be willing to let go of the past and embrace the present moment. This requires you to be fully present in each moment and to release the need to control or manipulate your experiences.

The journey of spiritual growth is a journey of awakening to your True Nature as a Divine being. It requires that you let go of the old stories and beliefs that no longer serve you, and to surrender to the Higher Self within you. As you do this, you begin to experience a deep sense of peace, joy, and interconnectedness with all of life.

The ego's grip on power seems so strong,
It fights the Truth to which we all belong.
It fears to lose control and must maintain,
Illusions of self with ego's refrain.

To grow spiritually we must let go,
Of patterns and beliefs that we do know
No longer serve us in our quest for Truth,
And keep us tied to ego's endless sleuth.

The work we do now is to realize
We're infinite consciousness in disguise.
Embodying within ourselves all good
And seeing it in others as we should.

But the ego resists a total good.
It fears it would dissolve misunderstood.
Thrives on control and manipulation,
It fights against its own liberation.

True spiritual growth requires us to see
Beyond ego's illusions and be free.
To trust the Higher Self and let it guide,
And shed the ego's chains that we once tied.

The Sparrow Sees Everything

The world seems more like a cage, especially as I go deeper into this dialogue. Is that accurate, that the world I perceive with my senses is like a cage or a straight jacket that keeps me from realizing who I really am?

I now open to the Master Teacher within and the Whole Mind that is forever my own.

Imagine a sparrow flying through an open window into a very large airport. Since the airport is so large it never finds its way back out to the "real world", but makes its home in the rafters of the airport. After some time it meets other sparrows who suffer the same captivity, and they form a community together. They talk about the other world they left, find mates and ultimately raise sparrow families. Generations pass and after many years the sparrows forget that there's a world outside the walls of the airport. They can see this larger world when they pass a window or even an open door, but the fear of what it means keeps them from leaving the world they've always known.

Then one of the sparrows, almost by accident, flies out through an open door and finds itself in the open air. At first the bird doesn't know how to react. It tries to fly back to "safety" but the door it flew through has closed. It looks through the glass at its sparrow friends and wonders if this is what death is - isolation.

As the days and weeks pass the sparrow wanders further and further from the airport. It sees huge steel birds that lift from the ground with a thunderous roar. It also meets other birds that are astounded by the sparrows stories of its "safe" home.

"Is it true that there's a ceiling that keeps you from soaring into the clouds," a hawks asks. "Are you telling me that the twigs and leaves you use to build your nests are made of plastic?" A crow inquires.

The sparrow begins to consider the possibility that it never knew what the real world was. As this idea and reality becomes more concrete it longs to find an open door so it can fly back into the airport building to tell his entire sparrow family its discovery. Then one day the sparrow meets a wise owl who helps the sparrow understand everything.

"The building where you lived was just as much a part of the real world as everything you're discovering now," the wise owl explains. "But you thought that the building where you lived was the only world and that everything you perceived outside the windows were fantasy. Your experience of the real world has expanded to include everything, not just some things. Your new vision allows you to perceive that which was always present but which was blocked by the walls within your own mind."

Think about this story. Are you the sparrow that's trapped inside the airport or the one flying through the open air? Be honest with yourself, and if you are able to admit that you're the one trapped inside the airport, what would it take to be free. The answer is simple - fly through the window that's being provided for you here.

A sparrow once flew through an airport wide,
And found a home within its vast inside,
Forgetting all the world it left behind,
It stayed with all the others of its kind.

The sparrows formed a community there,
And raised all their young with such tender care,
But as the generations passed them by,
They forgot the world far beyond the sky.

One day by chance the sparrow flew outside,
And saw the world with vision and wide-eyed,
Huge steel birds and other birds astounded,
By sparrow's tales of worlds he founded.

The sparrow began to long for much more,
To tell his family what he saw before,
But then a wise owl showed him how to see,
The airport was as real as all could be.

Walls in his mind had only blocked the view,
Of the real world he found forever true,
Expanding his vision beyond the walls,
That blessed sparrow then saw through it all.

No Such Thing As Without In Christ

I know people who claim that Christ or some other enlightened entity speaks through them. How can I know if this is true or just the person's imagination?

I now open to the Master Teacher within and the Whole Mind that is forever my own.

The Voice for Christ speaks through and for everyone, or it speaks through and for no one. If someone claims: "Jesus is speaking through me," or "I alone am the channel for this Voice," run away from them. Listen instead to the one who says: "Christ is speaking through YOU this and every moment no matter what your words or actions portray." This is the closest you can come to the experience of Christ within.

There is no such thing as "without" in Christ. Jesus knows this and that's why he could never participate in a "special" relationship. Specialness is really the desire to separate, to individually claim what is universally given. This is something Jesus, or the Christ, or any Whole Mind, would never do. The energy and wisdom of Christ is given to ALL because that is ALL it is and ALL that exists.

Does the Christ, or even Jesus, use other individuals to communicate its message of Oneness? Of course, but usually in a way that's not recognized by them. They simply feel something moving within them that erupts through a moment of revelation. When someone claims the identity of Jesus or anyone else in order to promote themselves, this is not the Christ and certainly not Jesus.

There have been those who have indeed heard and translated the voice of Christ, but they didn't do it in a self-promoting manner. The best example of this would be the consciousness that received A Course In Miracles. She questioned the authenticity of the Voice while having the tenacity to see the project through. For seven years she listened and transcribed my Voice, and when it was complete she was hesitant to share it with anyone. This is very different than someone claiming that Jesus or any other ascended being is speaking through them, then putting their own name on the book and claiming ownership. Are you able to see this?

Seek the voice for Christ where it is and will always remain - within you. And if anyone comes along claiming exclusive access to this great Voice, bless them and move on. Then (and this is the most important step) give away the same gift that you have received, and do so lavishly. A gift that is given totally can only be totally received, while a gift that has been given partially is no gift at all. Remember this and receive the Whole Gift that is being offered to you this and every moment.

The Voice for Christ speaks through and for everyone because it's the expression of the universal consciousness that's within us all. Christ is not exclusive to any one person or group of people, nor is it limited to any particular religion or spiritual tradition. The message of Christ is universal and is available to anyone who is willing to open themselves to it.

The ego, on the other hand, is always looking for ways to separate and divide, and it will use any means necessary to do so. That's why it's so important to be vigilant against the ego's attempts to claim ownership of the Voice for Christ. The ego wants to make the Voice for Christ exclusive, to limit it to certain individuals or groups, and to use it to promote its own agenda.

But the true Voice for Christ is always inclusive, always available to all, and always in service to the highest good of all. It's not interested in promoting any particular individual or group, but only in sharing the message of love and unity with all who are willing to receive it.

If you're seeking the Voice for Christ, look within yourself. This is where the True Voice can be found, not in any external source. When you're in tune with your inner guidance you'll be able to recognize the Voice for Christ in others as well.

Be aware that there are those who will claim to be the exclusive channel for the Voice for Christ. They may use this claim to gain power or to manipulate others. But the True Voice for Christ cannot be owned or controlled by any one person or group.

Remember that the message of Christ is one of love and inclusivity. It's not about promoting any particular person or group, but about bringing people together in a spirit of unity and compassion. When you hear the True Voice for Christ, you'll feel a sense of connection and oneness with all beings.

Be open to receiving the Voice for Christ in whatever form it comes to you. It may be a feeling, a thought, a dream, or an inner knowing. Trust that you'll be guided to the right people, places, and experiences that will help you to deepen your connection with the universal consciousness that is within you.

As you deepen your connection with the Voice for Christ, you'll begin to see the world in a new light. You'll see the interconnectedness of all things and the underlying unity that exists behind all appearances. You'll be filled with a sense of peace and joy that cannot be shaken by any external circumstances.

Remember that the Voice for Christ is always available to you, no matter where you are or what you're doing. It's not limited by time or space, and it's always present within you, waiting to be heard.

So if you're looking for the Voice for Christ, don't be swayed by those who claim to be its exclusive channel. Look within yourself and trust the guidance that comes from the universal consciousness that's within you. And remember to share the gift of the Voice for Christ with others so that they too may experience the peace and joy that comes from being in tune with the universal consciousness.

The Voice for Christ echoes in all of us,
Or none at all, such is its boundless reach,
All those who claim to be its chosen thus,
Deceive themselves, the truth they cannot teach.

Beware of those who claim the holy throne,
And say that Christ speaks solely through their voice,
For in their arrogance they stand alone,
And lead their followers to a fruitless choice.

But hearken to the one who speaks in love,
And says that Christ speaks through you every day,
Regardless of your thoughts or acts above,
His voice in every soul has found a way.

This truth alone can bring us closer still,
To the Divine that lies within us all,
And let us feel the love that He instills,
A light that shines beyond each mortal's wall.

Turn Your Gaze Toward the Real

The thought that I'll lose something if I accept everything seems ludicrous now, but that's the feeling that keeps us locked to the ego's dominance. Speak to me more about that.

I now open to the Master Teacher within and the Whole Mind that is forever my own.

Why spend so much time gazing at a world that never satisfies you or delivers on its promises? What has the material world ever promised you that became a consistent reality? The highest goal of everyone in perception seems to be dying in the arms of someone they love, or insulating themselves from sickness, pain and death by accumulating a long series of numbers in a bank account and the thin strips of paper those numbers seem to represent. Is this what you were made for?

No. This is not what you were made for. You were made for love alone since love created you perfect as Itself. Turn your gaze from what appears to be real to Reality itself. Only then will you feel the deep satisfaction you've lacked until now. This, in fact, is the only thing you've lacked - the deep satisfaction of Knowing you are whole and holy. You could never lack wholeness just as you could never be separated from the holiness at the very center of your being. The only thing you can lack is the knowledge of this wholeness, but this is a choice you've made on your own. No one forced you to look away from that which is all encompassing, as if such a thing were possible. No one asked you to forget the One who could never forget you, or could never stop loving you.

Turn your gaze from the without to the within, then the Kingdom of God will appear on its own.

The Kingdom of God is the only reality there is. It's here and now, always has been, and always will be. You're not separated from it, but only appear to be so. The world and everything in it are not the Kingdom of God, but merely a projection of your mind. The Kingdom of God is not something to be attained or achieved, but something to be remembered. It's the truth of who you are, the truth of your being.

To remember the Kingdom of God, you must first let go of all the false ideas and beliefs that you've been holding onto. These false ideas and beliefs are what keep you trapped in the illusion of separation, which is the cause of all your suffering. You must learn to see beyond this illusion to the truth that lies beyond it. You must learn to see the Kingdom of God within yourself and in others.

The only way to do this is through forgiveness. Forgiveness is the key to remembering the truth of who you are. It's the means by which you release all the false ideas and beliefs that you've been holding onto. Forgiveness is the way in which you let go of the past and open yourself to the present moment. It's the way in which you heal your mind and return to the truth of your being.

The Kingdom of God is not a place, but a state of mind. It's a state of consciousness in which you're aware of the truth of your being. It's a state of consciousness in which you're finally at peace, in which you're happy, in which you're free. The Kingdom of God is within you, waiting for you to remember it.

When you remember the Kingdom of God you'll see that everything in the world is a reflection of the truth of your being. You'll see that the world is not a place of suffering, but a place of healing. You'll see that everything in the world is here to help you remember the truth of who you are. You'll see that everything in the world is a gift from God.

Turn your gaze from the without to the within, and let the Kingdom of God appear on its own. Let go of all the false ideas and beliefs that have kept you trapped in the illusion of separation. Forgive yourself and others for all the perceived wrongs and let the truth of your being shine through. You were made for love alone, and that love is the only reality there is.

Nothing is lost when you share what is true. You cannot give anything away since loss is as unreal as the world you created in your imagination to hide from Reality. All you can do is share, knowing that through sharing the blessings that have been given to you so freely, they return to the Source which is within you now. The Source of all love, light and Grace is who you are, but to experience this you must be willing to give away the love that created you.

Begin now. Give everything then you'll know that everything of true value rests within you now and forever.

Why chase after a world that brings no peace,
And fails to keep the promises it makes?
Its offerings can only give release,
In fleeting moments that soon turn to breaks.

Your goal, to die in someone's warm embrace,
Or gather riches to ward off all strife,
Is not what gives your heart a lasting Grace,
Or fills your soul with the eternal life.

For you were made in love, pure and Divine,
And in that love alone you will find rest,
That will not fade or wither with all time,
But grow so full and deep within your chest.

So turn your gaze from this world's fleeting charms,
And seek the love that fills eternal arms.

The Problem and the Solution

This conversation has helped me stop looking at the so-called problems in my life and see only the Real expanding further and further. I never actually understood the problem or the solution, but the more I let all my attachments dissolve, the solution appears on its own.

I now open to the Master Teacher within and the Whole Mind that is forever my own.

It's true, neither the problem nor the solution is where you think they are. People will say: "This is where you should look," or "That's whom we should blame." Don't listen to any of them. The problem and the solution are both in YOUR mind, nowhere else. Heal your mind and the world you perceive is automatically healed. (Don't be alarmed by this. There is only ONE Mind and the idea that your mind is separate from ALL minds is the only problem you have.) It is only there that it can be healed.

Others may call you insensitive and disconnected. They'll say you don't care about what's happening to other people, but you'll respond by saying: "I care TOTALLY, and that is why I AM."

This is not a riddle for you to figure out in your mind, but a reality to be embraced by your soul. Embrace it now and you'll realize that you never left your home and that God's love has never been compromised. When you see the world as broken and in need of fixing it's easy to fall into despair and hopelessness. But the truth is that the world is perfect as it is, and the only thing that needs to change is your perception of it. When you recognize that the problem and the solution are in your own mind, you become empowered to effect real change.

It can be difficult to accept that the source of your suffering is not outside of you, but within. It's much easier to blame others for your problems and to seek external solutions. But true healing requires a radical shift in perspective. When you take responsibility for your own thoughts and beliefs you can begin to transform them and create a better world.

The world may appear to be a chaotic and unpredictable place, but in truth, it's a reflection of your own thoughts and beliefs. When you heal your mind, you change the world you see. This is not a passive process, but an active one. It requires courage, commitment, and a willingness to face your own darkness. When you embrace the idea that the problem and the solution are in your own mind, you become a powerful force for change. You no longer need to wait for others to fix the world or for circumstances to change. You can begin to transform the world right now, at this moment, by changing your own mind.

This is not to say that you should ignore the suffering of others or turn a blind eye to injustice. On the contrary, when you heal your own mind you become more compassionate, more loving, and more effective in your efforts to help others. Your actions become a natural expression of your true nature, rather than a reaction to external circumstances.

When you recognize that the problem and the solution are in your own mind you become a true agent of change. You no longer need to wait for permission or for the right circumstances. You can begin to transform the world right now, simply by changing your mind about the world.

Don't listen to those who tell you that the problem is outside of you. Don't be swayed by those who say that the solution is beyond your reach. The truth is that the problem and the solution are both within, waiting for you to claim them.

Problems and solutions do not exist
Where others say they do, so don't persist
To look outside yourself for answers clear
For what you seek within will thus appear

The world you see is but a reflection
Of thoughts and beliefs, a mere projection
Of what is held within your very mind
So search within and the world will be kind

Some may accuse you of some apathy
And say you lack compassion's empathy
But you know that to truly care and love
Is to seek the truth from Whole Mind above

For in that space of Oneness and pure Light
You'll find the love that makes everything right
And in your caring for yourself and all
You'll heal the world both wholly great and small

Look With Soft Eyes

I'm beginning to relax my grip on everything. It feels strange sometimes, almost like I don't care anymore, but what I'm discovering is that I care totally. A total expression of love is entering my mind and flowing through my life. Does this make sense?

I now open to the Master Teacher within and the Whole Mind that is forever my own.

Let your hold on the world loosen as the Real World begins to take shape in your mind. Look softly upon everyone you meet, no matter what the circumstances might be, and you'll perceive a bright light, like a creative pulse, that leads you away from the world you've known until now into the Heaven you never really left.

As you begin to see the creative force behind everything, you'll realize that the world you've known until now is nothing but a projection of your thoughts. I know I've said this many times already but it's the only lesson left for you to learn. Learn it NOW since this is the time you chose. There is no other time but this. This is the moment for your spirit to finally fly above and beyond this strange world. Spread your wings and let the breath of God take you.

It's in this world of spirit that you'll find true joy and happiness. It's not in the accumulation of things, or in the acquisition of knowledge or power. It's in the simple act of being present in the moment, fully aware of the love that surrounds you.

As you become more and more aware of the love that surrounds you, you'll begin to see that all creation is connected. There's no separation between you and the world around you. You're one with everything that exists. This realization will soon bring you great peace and comfort.

It's in this state of peace and comfort that you'll find the courage to let go of the things that once held you captive. You'll begin to see that the things you once held dear were nothing but illusions, and that the true beauty of life lies in the simplicity of being.

So let go of the illusions that have held you captive. Let go of the things that once seemed so important. Embrace the true beauty of life, which lies in the simplicity of Being. Know that you're one with everything that exists, and that the love that surrounds you is eternal.

As you embrace this truth, you'll begin to see the world in a new light. You'll see the beauty that's always been there, but that you were once blind to. You'll see the interconnectedness of all things, and you'll know that everything is perfect just the way it is.

Let your hold on the world be tenuous. Look with soft eyes upon all created things and you'll begin to perceive the creative force behind everything. Relax and know that you are one with everything that exists, and that the love that surrounds you is eternal.

As you begin to see beyond the veil,
You'll find the world you knew was but a tale,
A mere projection of the thoughts you hold,
A world of mere illusions, bright and bold.

The true world lies in Spirit's loving light,
Where love and joy forever reign in sight,
No joy can come from power, wealth, or gain,
True bliss can only come from what's the same.

Be present in the moment, fully aware,
Of love and light that constantly ensnare,
Embrace the world of spirit and its Grace,
And in its loving arms find your true place.

Nothing But God

The perceptual world seems to be based on the need to "get" things I don't already possess which will change my life in some way. I now see that there's nothing the world can give me of real value that's not already within. This seems to be the essence of everything being expressed here, yes?

I now open to the Master Teacher within and the Whole Mind that is forever my own.

When will you stop seeking anything other than God? When you finally realize that there is nothing but God you'll know that there's nothing left to seek. This is the only goal left to achieve, the realization that there's nothing in all the Universe but this Universal Love we call God. It's not an entity we seek but a Reality that's forever Real. It's not an image we desire but that which exists beyond all earthly desires. The earth and everything in it disappear in this Grace. You're left with nothing but love, for love is all there is.

To experience this love, you must let go of all that is not love. This means letting go of all that is egoic, all that is selfish, all that is based on fear, and all that is not pure and true. It means allowing the love within you to shine forth, unobstructed by the limited perceptions of the world. It means seeing past the illusions of separation, seeing beyond the differences that seem to divide us, and recognizing the Oneness that unites us all.

When you realize that there is nothing but God, you begin to see everything as an expression of God's love. Every moment, every breath, and every experience is an opportunity to connect with this love and share it with others. You realize that your purpose in life is not to accumulate wealth, power, or status, but to embody the love of God and spread it wherever you go.

This is not an easy task. It requires courage, faith, and a deep commitment to the truth. It means facing your fears and doubts, acknowledging your limitations, and surrendering to the unknown. It means trusting that God's love will guide you every step of the way.

But once you take this leap of faith, once you surrender to God's love, you'll experience a profound sense of peace, joy and fulfillment. You'll no longer feel lost, alone or disconnected from the world around you. You'll know that you're loved, that you're a part of something greater than yourself, and that your life has a purpose that transcends all understanding.

Let go of all that is not love. Open your heart to the love of God and let it transform you from the inside out. Let it guide you to the realization that there's nothing but God, and that this is the only truth worth seeking. When you do, you'll find the peace, joy, and fulfillment that you've been searching for all along.

Remember, you are not separate from God, but rather an expression of God's love. You're not a victim of circumstances, but a co-creator of your own reality. You're not limited by your past, but free to create a new future. You are not alone, but surrounded by a vast network of loving beings who are here to support and guide you on your journey.

Take a deep breath, let go of all that is not love, and embrace the Truth that there is nothing but love. You're here to experience and express this love, to share it with

others, and to help create a world that reflects the infinite beauty and majesty of the Divine. This is your purpose, your destiny, and your birthright. Embrace it fully, and you'll know true happiness, true fulfillment, and true peace.

Release all the fears and doubts that bind you,
Release the pain that keeps you trapped in time,
And trust that love will guide you to the truth,
Where peace and joy and freedom are Divine.

The search for God is not a journey far,
But simply turning inward to the Source.
For in the silence of the heart you are
The very Love that you have longed to course.

So rest in Love, and let the world recede.
For in the stillness you will surely find
That you are Love and everything you need
Is here within the Presence of your Mind.

Master's Last Words

I know that there's no end to this journey, but I'm wondering if there's anything left that hasn't been shared yet, anything that will lead to a final discovery of Grace within?

I now open to the Master Teacher within and the Whole Mind that is forever my own.

There's nothing left to say. In fact, there was never anything to say other than YES, I AM HERE. Anything else is a reduction. Anything more is impossible. God, or the essence of love itself, is calling you to an intimate experience and expression of NOW. Nothing has ever been said, or could ever be said, that will change this.

God is calling you to THIS moment, and in this moment you have a choice. Will you affirm that which has always affirmed you? Or will you continue to deny that which could never deny you? This is the essence of your freedom, your freedom of choice. But you cannot really choose what has never been real. You can create the illusion of choosing what could never be, but this is not a real choice. The only real choice is love because love is the only thing that is real. It really is that simple.

Choosing love is not always easy though, as it may require you to let go of old beliefs and patterns that no longer serve you. It may require you to step out of your comfort zone and into the unknown. But it's only in the unknown that true growth and transformation can occur.

When you say YES to love, you're saying YES to the infinite possibilities of the universe. You're saying YES to a life of abundance, joy, and peace. You're saying YES to the beauty and wonder of creation, and to the power and intelligence that guides it.

Saying YES to love means trusting the Divine plan and surrendering to the flow of life. It means releasing the need to control every aspect of your life and trusting that everything is unfolding in perfect timing and in perfect order.

Love is not a passive state. It's an active one. It requires you to be fully present in each moment, to be aware of your thoughts and actions, and to choose love over fear, judgment, and separation. When you choose love, you become a channel for the Divine energy to flow through you into the world. You become a vehicle for the expression of God's love and wisdom, and a beacon of light in a world so often dark and chaotic.

Choosing love is not just a one-time decision, but a continuous practice. It requires daily discipline, devotion, and commitment. It requires you to be willing to forgive yourself and others, to let go of grievances and resentments, and to see everyone as a reflection of the Divine.

Through the practice of love, you come to know yourself and others as one. You come to see the interconnectedness of all things and the unity that underlies all creation. You come to realize that there's no separation, only the illusion of it.

In the end, there really is nothing left to say, for love speaks for itself. It is the essence of who you are and the answer to all your questions. It's the force that holds the universe together and the glue that binds us all. So say

YES to love, and watch as your life transforms in ways you could never have imagined.

In the end, words fall short of love's embrace,
For love speaks for itself in every space.
It is the answer to life's deepest quests,
The force that holds the universe at rest.

With love as the essence of who you are,
Your questions find answers that heal and star,
It binds us all like a powerful glue,
Transforming your life into a world that's new.

So say YES to love in every way,
And watch now as it guides you day by day.
With true love as your guide, you'll never stray,
For this love is the path to an eternal stay.

Join James Twyman Five Days a Week

Did you know that James shares new *Master Teacher Within* lessons Monday - Friday LIVE on Zoom? Namaste Village in Ajijic, Mexico offers these sessions so thousands of people around the world can continue their ascent into Whole-mindedness. To receive the link, make sure you're on James's email list. Visit www.JamesFTwyman.com and look for the link toward the top of the page. This is the best way to tap into the Master Teacher within you. Make sure you also check out www.Namaste-Village.com and www.I-Am-Awake.com for more exciting programs and opportunities.

Made in the USA
Las Vegas, NV
18 April 2023

70739807R00125